Wally Caruana
graduated in Fine Arts from the
Canberra School of Art in 1975, and is presently
Curator of Aboriginal Art at the National Gallery
of Australia, Canberra. He has curated a number of
exhibitions, and edited the volume *Windows on the
Dreaming, Aboriginal Paintings in the Australian
National Gallery*, published in 1989.

WORLD OF ART

This famous series
provides the widest available
range of illustrated books on art in all its aspects.
If you would like to receive a complete list
of titles in print please write to:
THAMES AND HUDSON
30 Bloomsbury Street, London WC1B 3QP
In the United States please write to:
THAMES AND HUDSON INC.
500 Fifth Avenue, New York, New York 10110

Printed in Singapore

WALLY CARUANA

ABORIGINAL ART

187 illustrations, 31 in color

THAMES AND HUDSON

To Stephanie and Michael, and in memory of Jack Wunuwun

Frontispiece:
1 Jack Wunuwun, *Banumbirr the Morning Star*, 1987 (see p.54)

The publishers wish to express their gratitude for the
co-operation of the National Gallery of Australia in the
preparation of this volume.

First published in the United States of America in 1993 by
Thames and Hudson Inc., 500 Fifth Avenue,
New York, New York 10110
Reprinted 1995

Library of Congress Catalog Card Number 92-62140
ISBN 0-500-20264-8

Printed and bound in Singapore

Contents

CHAPTER ONE

Introduction

The art of Aboriginal Australia is the last great tradition of art to be appreciated by the world at large. Despite being one of the longest continuous traditions of art in the world, dating back at least fifty millennia, it remained relatively unknown until the second half of the twentieth century. The Surrealist map of the world, published in 1929 by the Parisian avant-garde, depicted the size of each country proportionate to the degree of artistic creativity, with the recently discovered riches of the Pacific islands looming large. Australia barely featured.

The often ephemeral materials of Aboriginal art make it difficult to determine the antiquity of the majority of the forms of art practised today. The most durable forms are the multitudes of rock engravings and rock paintings which are found across the continent. In the Arnhem Land escarpment evidence suggests that paintings were being made fifty thousand years ago, antedating the Palaeolithic rock paintings of Altamira and Lascaux in Europe. Engraved designs found in South Australia have been dated to at least thirty thousand years before the present. More recent dates for engravings and paintings at these and other art sites indicate continuous artistic activity over the millennia.

The first inhabitants of the continent arrived from the north and spread across the land to populate a range of environments, which today include the tropical regions of the north and the temperate climates of the south, harsh deserts and fertile river lands. With little contact from the rest of the world, cultural practices spread across the country, developing a diversity which is reflected in the variety of religious beliefs, ceremonies, social structures, languages (in pre-European times over two hundred distinct languages and many more dialects were spoken, although only about fifty are in daily use now), and in particular, in the range of artistic practices and idioms.

Art is central to Aboriginal life. Whether it is made for political, social, utilitarian or didactic purposes – and these functions constantly overlap – art is inherently connected to the religious domain.

7

◀ 2 Rock painting, Kakadu, Northern Territory

orres Strait
Islands
● Erub (Darnley Island)

Weipa

kun
ape
York
Peninsula
Cape
veer

Laura ●

Cairns ●

QUEENSLAND

SOUTH

PACIFIC

OCEAN

Fraser Island

Brisbane ●

NEW SOUTH WALES

rray R

Sydney ●
Wilton

Canberra ●

KE
RRELL

ICTORIA

Melbourne ● ● Coranderrk

Flinders Island

ount
on West

Hobart ● TASMANIA

Milikapati   Cobourg Peninsula   Minjilang (Croker Island)
Bathurst   Maningrida   Galiwinku
Island   Melville Island   Milingimbi (Elcho Island)
       Nguiu   Gunbalanya   Ramingining
                             (Oenpelli)   Yirrkala
       Darwin   Gurka'wuy R   Trial Bay
             Kadadu   Blue Mud Bay
             National Park   Liverpool R   Chasm Island
                                                    Koolatong R
Wadeye   ARNHEM   Groote
(Port Keats)   LAND   Eylandt
        Kimul   Daly R   Bickerton
                                  Jarruluk   Island
   Fitzmaurice R   Katherine R   Roper R
                                     Ngukurr   Limmen Bight
         Victoria R

E Alligator R
Mann R
Tor ison R
Cadell R
Blyth R

3 Map of Australia showing major
and representative locations referred
to in the text

Art is a means by which the present is connected with the past and human beings with the supernatural world. Art activates the powers of the ancestral beings. Art expresses individual and group identity, and the relationships between people and the land.

Until the advent of Europeans to Australia in the eighteenth century, Aboriginal art was made purely to fulfil traditional cultural needs, and this has remained the case in varying degrees since. In the ceremonial sphere, art may only be created and viewed by those initiated to the proper level of awareness. However, in modern times, a significant body of art has emerged which is intended for the wider, public domain.

THE DREAMING

The religious life of Aboriginal people centres on the Dreaming. The Dreaming is a European term used by Aborigines to describe the spiritual, natural and moral order of the cosmos. It relates to the period from the genesis of the universe to a time beyond living memory. The period is also known as the Dreamtime. The terms do not refer to the state of dreams or unreality, but rather to a state of a reality beyond the mundane. The Dreaming focuses on the activities and epic deeds of the supernatural beings and creator ancestors such as the Rainbow Serpents, the Lightning Men, the Wagilag Sisters, the Tingari and Wandjina, who, in both human and non-human form, travelled across the unshaped world, creating everything in it and laying down the laws of social and religious behaviour. The Dreaming is not, however, merely a guide for living, an agent of social control, or simply a chronicle of creation, restricted in time to a definable past. The Dreaming provides the ideological framework by which human society retains a harmonious equilibrium with the universe – a charter and mandate that has been sanctified over time.

The continent of Australia is covered by an intricate web of Dreamings. Some relate to a particular place or region and belong to those who reside there, other Dreamings travel over vast distances and connect those whose lands they cover. Thus people may be connected to several Dreamings. The all-pervasive powers of the ancestral beings of the Dreamings are present in the land and in natural species, and also reside within individuals. They are activated by ceremony and art to nourish generation after generation of human descendants. An individual's links with the ancestral beings in the Dreaming, and his or her spiritual identity, are expressed through totemic associations with natural species and phenomena, ritual songs, dances, objects and graphic designs. The events of the Dreaming provide the great themes of Aboriginal art.

Aboriginal visual art takes many forms, from the enduring rock engravings and paintings to the more ephemeral arts of body decoration, bark and ground paintings and ceremonial sculpture in wood. Ritual and utilitarian objects are made from stone, wood, paint, woven fibre and feathers, and jewellery is also made from bone, shell and seeds. Regional variations abound; in Arnhem Land paintings on flattened sheets of bark are common, whereas ground paintings are made in the desert. Although most traditional forms, ground paintings for example, continue to be largely restricted to ceremonial use, others, such as painting on bark and wood sculpture readily fulful ritual functions and are made for the public domain as well. Recent years have witnessed the flourishing of some art forms and the demise of others. The adoption of new technologies and materials such as canvas and synthetic paints has led to the creation of new art forms which often complement rather than replace existing ones.

4–9

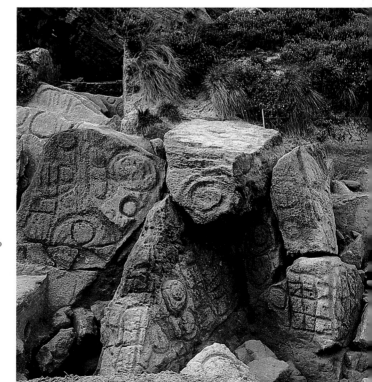

4 Rock engraving, *c.* AD 500, Mount Cameron West, Tasmania

5–6 Rock art, Northern Territory: (*left*) Lightning Brothers and lightning figures, Katherine River. (*below, far left*) Hand stencil, Kakadu, 9–20,000 years before the present

7 (*below left*) Narrative rock painting, Musgrave Ranges, South Australia

8 (*right*) Bradshaw figures, rock painting, the Kimberley, *c.* 3,000 years before the present

9 (*below*) Rock drawing of kangaroos, Wilton, New South Wales

Aboriginal Australia embraces a number of distinct classical or long-established artistic traditions within which conventional graphic designs and representational symbols are the most potent, but far from exclusive, carriers of meaning. Each artistic idiom contains a lexicon of designs and symbols which may be used in a multitude of combinations and contexts. Unlike prose, the interpretation of Aboriginal designs and images is not a one-to-one equivalence. Rather, like poetry with all its inherent complexities, multiple references and intended ambiguities, each symbol or icon within a work may encapsulate a variety of meanings.

Each set of designs is interpreted according to the ritual, social and political situations in which it is presented. The levels of interpretation of an image or design depend on the ritual knowledge of both artist and viewer, and on an understanding of the ancestral landscape. Thus a ritually senior man will have access to a broad range of meanings of a particular image. He may elaborate on these in describing works created for ceremony, whereas in a work made for the education of an uninitiated youth, or for public display, he will confine his account to the appropriate level or levels of interpretation. Today it is common practice for artists to provide a description of their work, and the many levels of interpretation permit artists to present their art to an often culturally untutored public without compromising its religious nature. Artists talk of two broad levels of interpretation, the 'inside' stories which are restricted to those of the appropriate ritual standing, and the 'outside' stories which are open to all.

Meaning is elaborated in terms of spiritual power. Religious images and designs, when applied to any surface, whether the body of a participant in ritual or the surface of a shield or a carrying bag, have the power to transform the nature of the thing from a mundane state to an extraordinary one, from the profane to the sacred. In ceremony, people's bodies and objects are taken from a dull state to one of brilliance by the application of paint and designs. The concept of brightness often carries through into art intended for the public domain: not only does it evoke the radiant presence of supernatural power but it also provides a means by which artists explore concepts beyond the tangible qualities of life.

ART AND AUTHORITY

It is by the acquisition of knowledge, not material possessions, that one attains status in Aboriginal culture. Art is an expression of knowledge, and hence a statement of authority. Through the use of ancestrally inherited designs, artists assert their identity, and their rights and responsibilities. They also define the relationships between individuals and groups, and affirm their connections to the land and the Dreaming.

Traditional Aboriginal society is structured by a number of systems that organize all aspects of life and perceptions, and, indeed, by which the universe is ordered. The systems vary in detail from society to society but include kin groups and 'moieties'. An individual is placed in one of up to eight kinship groups, while people and all the phenomena of the natural and spiritual worlds are classed as belonging to one or other of two complementary groups, the moieties. Jointly these affiliations determine a person's conduct in every aspect of social and religious behaviour. Marriage, for example, is customarily conducted between members of specific kinship groups belonging to opposite moieties. In art, moiety affiliation plays an important role in determining the subjects to which an artist has access and, in many cases, the manner in which they are depicted.

Individuals inherit through their parents both direct and indirect rights and responsibilities to land, ceremonies and Dreamings, as well as their connections to the ancestral and supernatural beings. Those with direct rights in a ceremony or Dreaming – today mostly derived through patrilineal inheritance – are termed the owners. They, however, do not activate or control the ritual but work in conjunction with those of the opposite moiety who have secondary or indirect rights in the ceremony, derived through matrilineal descent. Members of the latter group are often called the managers or workers, and they create ritual art in negotiation with and under the supervision of the owners. The roles of individuals vary according to the ceremony being performed. Thus ceremonial activity (including art) requires cooperation between the two groups in a specified relationship to each other.

The regulations which apply to the ownership of and rights to land and Dreamings in traditional societies are, with varying degrees of modification, carried over into the making of art for the public domain. An individual artist to whom a work is attributed will be the owner of, or have other rights to depict the subject. In this way, the prerogatives of artists to use sacred designs and to depict religious subjects are regulated. Ownership of the designs is akin to copyright over them; the use of designs belonging to others without the appropriate permission constitutes a major breach of Aboriginal law.

This issue assumes greater significance in a world where the designs are broadcast much more widely than ever before.

As a statement of authority, the aesthetic in art is often articulated in terms of ritual knowledge. Through art, individuals express their authority and knowledge of a subject, the land and the Dreaming, and artists will use their authority to introduce change and innovation. It is their authority that artists bring to bear in their relationships with the world at large. Through art, they express the relevance of their culture to a world that has neglected or attempted to undermine Aboriginal values.

THE LAST TWO CENTURIES

In addition to the cultural differences between Aboriginal groups, Aboriginal society today encompasses people with vastly different historic experiences, particularly over the last two centuries. While Aboriginal cultures across the country possess uniting principles and common features, they are not static; they have been and continue to be dynamic societies, capable of responding to both internal and external influences. These include dramatic environmental changes over the millennia as well as the great trauma induced by the recent settlement of Australia by Europeans.

Despite the fact that the Aboriginal population probably numbered about a million in 1788, the continent of Australia was declared *terra nullius*, the empty land, by the early British settlers, thus sidestepping claims to sovereignty by Aboriginal people and permitting the wholesale takeover of the country. With few exceptions, Aboriginal people, their beliefs, customs and land were treated with scant respect by the invaders. In many parts of the continent, the original inhabitants were forced from their homes, denied access to natural resources, and witnessed the dismemberment of their society. While the British met with a great degree of resistance in the form of battles and guerilla warfare, the cultural and social dispossession of the Aboriginal people had commenced. The nineteenth century saw the settlement of large parts of the continent.

In the first years of the twentieth century, Australia's newly formed federal government introduced institutionalized racism under the policies of assimilation. In essence, assimilation declared the discrete Aboriginal culture redundant, and sought to submerge Aboriginal Australians in what was considered to be, in the Darwinian sense, the dominant society.

16

Nevertheless, Aboriginal people across Australia have striven to maintain their identity. In the 1930s Aboriginal people began to organize themselves politically, and through demonstrations and petitions demanded equality and the social and political rights that had been denied them. By the 1960s, the Aboriginal struggle gained momentum with the first concerted land rights claims and the establishment of organizations for social advancement. Official recognition of rights to land was high on the Aboriginal agenda, the centrality of land to Aboriginal social and religious life being paramount.

In 1963, North East Arnhem Land people used art as a means of expressing to the world the nature of their attachment to the land; bark paintings were submitted as evidence of legal title to their land to the Australian Government in constitutional procedures concerning Aboriginal land rights. It was not until 1976, however, that land rights legislation of any form was finally enacted in the Northern Territory.

In 1967 universal suffrage for Aboriginal people became a reality and in 1972 the Aboriginal campaign brought about fundamental changes in official government policy; the assimilation policies were revoked in recognition of the demands for self-determination for Aboriginal people. For the first time in two centuries Aboriginal people had a voice in the running of their own affairs. With increased political freedoms came the gradual acknowledgment of some Aboriginal rights to land, and the opening up of social and economic opportunities. These advances, however, are yet to manifest themselves in every aspect of social and political life across the country. Genuine social justice and equality are still far from a reality, and the struggle continues. Nonetheless, as people expressed pride in their culture, and many resumed a fuller traditional and ceremonial life, art again began to flourish. The strength of Aboriginal culture today is testimony to the resilience and determination of the Aboriginal people.

ART IN THE PUBLIC DOMAIN

The achievements of Aboriginal artists are now well regarded, but European attitudes were not always so sympathetic. The first European visitors to the shores of Australia made note of the cultural artefacts they encountered; their paintings, drawings and engravings of the period illustrate Aboriginal weapons and implements, and 10 show people with their bodies covered in painted designs. In

10 George French Angus, *Native weapons and implements*, 1847

Tasmania in 1802, the Baudin expedition found a shelter of bark sheets decorated with designs scratched into their blackened surfaces. The British saw mortuary structures on Melville Island in 1824. Rock art sites were recorded. These manifestations of Aboriginal culture were not seen as art, however, but as ethnographic evidence. Nineteenth-century attitudes placed Aboriginal Australians on the lowest rung of the evolutionary ladder, and they were regarded as a people without art.

Aboriginal artefacts had been collected by many of the early explorers and settlers and, indeed, some collections were sent to scientific museums in Europe. A number of those that remained in Australia were eventually housed in local museums of natural history, where they shared the space with geological, plant and animal specimens, reflecting contemporary attitudes. Colonial governments also made collections intended for the great International Exhibitions of Europe, where Aboriginal artefacts were used either for decoration or as examples of the curious manufacture of a colonized culture. It was only in the latter half of the century, with the beginning of serious anthropological interest, that Aboriginal people began to be seen to have complex religious structures around which their societies were built, and their cultural products to possess intrinsic merit as expressions of their perceptions of the universe.

A notable step was the first exhibition of Aboriginal art, *Dawn of Art*, held in Adelaide in the late 1880s. It contained drawings on paper made by Aboriginal prisoners, and possibly staff, at Palmerston jail, in what is now the city of Darwin. The subjects of these drawings are naturalistically rendered animals with bodies decorated in a similar manner to the rock art of northern Australia.

The first major exhibition to feature Aboriginal art, *Primitive Art*, was organized in 1929 by the National Museum of Victoria. The exhibition included bark paintings collected in 1912 by Baldwin Spencer, a former director of the Museum, whose collections and writings did much to promote Aboriginal art.

In 1941 and 1942, the exhibition *Art of Australia 1788–1941* was the first to present Aboriginal art in an artistic context internationally, touring the United States and Canada, although the inclusion of three drawings by Tommy McRae and eleven Northern Territory bark paintings was intended to represent the local forerunners to art in the European tradition in Australia.

Also in 1941, an exhibition in Sydney featured Aboriginal artefacts along with the work of non-Aboriginal painters and decorative artists using Aboriginal designs or depicting Aboriginal subjects. It heralded a growing awareness of Aboriginal art, although it misguidedly proclaimed its appropriation to foster a unique Australian artistic identity.

After World War II, the growth of anthropological studies and an increasing interest in some quarters of the Australian art world led to a greater appreciation of Aboriginal art. Items from the ethnologist Charles Mountford's major government-sponsored field collection of 1948 in Arnhem Land were later distributed among the state art museums. In 1957–8, Mountford organized an exhibition of bark paintings which toured Europe.

Among the several exhibitions of the 1950s, *The Art of Arnhem Land*, curated by the anthropologists Ronald and Catherine Berndt in 1957, was significant in that it was the first to situate identified artists within stylistic traditions. By 1959 the Art Gallery of New South

Wales actively pursued the acquisition of a collection of contemporary works through the efforts of a curator at the Gallery, Tony Tuckson, who was also an artist, and the private collector Stuart Scougall. This collection toured Australia in the following year, and signalled the beginnings of the wider acceptance of Aboriginal art. Aboriginal art is now an integral part of the collections of the national and state art museums of the country.

The present level of awareness of Aboriginal art also owes significantly to the efforts of those non-Aboriginal people who have lived and worked in communities and promoted the understanding of Aboriginal culture further afield. The genuine interest in art shown by a number of missionaries, schoolteachers, social workers and government officials – from Pastor Johann Reuther at Lake Eyre in 1903 to Geoffrey Bardon at Papunya in 1971–2, and many others in more recent times – has encouraged artists to produce work for an outside audience.

The interest in Aboriginal art which began in the 1960s has created new opportunities for Aboriginal artists, as their work leaves the communities to be shown in cities and towns across Australia and overseas. Today Aboriginal art is represented with increasing regularity in major exhibitions and hangs in public and private collections both locally and internationally. Meanwhile, the imperatives to produce art for traditional purposes continue, and the expanded environment in which Aboriginal art operates has created further compelling reasons for Aboriginal artists to express the values of their culture to the wider world in which they live.

The following chapters are organized along regional lines to introduce the scope and vitality of Aboriginal visual art across the country. They survey the major art areas of Aboriginal Australia, looking back to some of the early and more recent examples of art, and examine the continuing and evolving traditions as they are seen today in all their diversity, from the bark paintings of Arnhem Land, the canvases of the desert and the Kimberley, the sculptures of northern Queensland, to the variety of media and techniques used by artists from cities and towns, and more besides.

CHAPTER TWO

Patterns of power: Arnhem Land and its surrounds

In the tropical north, Arnhem Land and the adjacent areas represent one of the richest art-producing regions of the country. Covering an area of approximately 150,000 square kilometres, Arnhem Land encompasses a range of environments, from the great sandstone plateau in the west with its thousands of galleries of magnificent rock paintings, to countless rivers, freshwater lagoons, monsoon jungles, open forests, rugged stone areas, mud-flats, coastal lands and islands.

    Of the portable arts, Arnhem Land is renowned for bark painting, sculptures and weaving, with a variation in emphasis and styles across the region. In general the paintings of the west tend towards the figurative, and as one moves east, geometric designs become more prominent. On Groote Eylandt, bark paintings are characterized by the black grounds against which the images are set, while around Ngukurr, artists today prefer to use bright acrylic paints on canvas to relate the Dreamings. The Tiwi of Bathurst and Melville Islands produce vigorous sculptures in ironwood, while the art of Wadeye and Kimul displays influences of desert culture.

    Apart from the traditional communications between groups in and adjacent to Arnhem Land, the earliest evidence of regular external contact in the region dates back three or four centuries to Macassan fishermen from Sulawesi in Indonesia who came in search of trepang (sea-cucumber), a highly-prized delicacy in China. While they did not settle, the Macassans had some influence on the cosmology and technology of the local peoples.

    Sustained contact with Europeans began with tentative attempts by the British to settle on Melville Island in 1824, and on the nearby mainland in the following years. The first permanent settlement, Palmerston (later Darwin), was founded in the second half of the nineteenth century. Over the next one hundred years settlements and missions were established in Arnhem Land which was declared a reserve for Aboriginal people in 1931. In recent decades, these settlements have become Aboriginal towns and service centres for the many people who have moved back to live on their clan lands. This so-called homelands or outstation movement has stimulated an increase in ceremonial and traditional activity, while a drive for a degree of economic independence accelerated the production of art for the public domain. The towns have developed artists' cooperatives or art centres which have become conduits for the movement of art from the region to the outside world.

While several distinct languages are spoken across Arnhem Land, each as different from the other as say, French is from Russian, the peoples of the region have similar forms of social organization and hold many religious beliefs and ceremonies in common.

The complex social structures which organize religious and secular life and articulate the relationships to ancestral beings, ceremonies and Dreamings are reflected in art. Many Dreaming stories originate in one area and travel across the region, assuming a wider significance as they link clans who are associated with them. Especially prominent among these are the Dreamings concerning the ancestral beings 16, 34 Yingarna and Ngalyod the Rainbow Serpents, the Wagilag Sisters, 44 the Djang'kawu, and Barama and Lany'tjung, all of whom figure in 52 major ceremonial cycles.

The immense sandstone plateau which rises above the surrounding lowlands in western Arnhem Land contains the galleries of spectacular rock art. Archaeological evidence suggests that paintings were being made some fifty thousand years ago. The oldest paintings in existence are believed to be at least eighteen thousand years old, created during the Ice Age when the sea was well below its present level. Studies of the environmental changes that have occurred since this period, and the changes in styles and motifs, along with the sequences of superimposed images, have enabled archaeologists broadly to determine the temporal sequence in this art. The earliest 6 images are imprints of hands, plants and bundles of string thrown against the wall. These were followed by naturalistic monochrome images of animals and humans in animated postures in a style previously known as 'mimi', after the spirit figures they represent, and now commonly called the 'dynamic style' of rock painting.

Nearly ten thousand years ago, as the sea level rose and the coastal environment came closer to the escarpment, marine creatures began 2 to feature in rock paintings. Rainbow Serpents, creator-beings associated with water, made their appearance. It is estimated that polychrome figures with internal anatomical details visible, in what is now known as the 'x-ray style', were introduced in the last three thousand years. The most recent periods of rock painting portray

22

11 Najombolmi, rock painting of *Hunter*, 1960s

scenes and images relating to contact with the Macassans and later with Europeans.

The rock art tradition has continued into the twentieth century. One of the most prolific and well known Kakadu rock painters of the modern era was Najombolmi, also known as Barramundi Charlie, whose elaborate animated *mimi* spirit figure is depicted here throwing a spear. Ritual ornaments hang from his elbows and neck. Working in the last years of his life, Najombolmi has superimposed this image over earlier paintings.

11

23

Characteristically, artists like Najombolmi work in more than one medium, although some artists are renowned as specialists in a particular form. The establishment of a market for art outside the communities has encouraged artists to specialize. Since the early 1900s the demands of anthropologists, researchers and collectors for portable works of art have stimulated the production of bark paintings, although the entire Arnhem Land region is also rich in other forms of art including painted wood sculpture and dyed and woven natural fibres which often incorporate feathers.

Bark is a perishable material and the antiquity of the tradition of bark painting is difficult to establish. The practice of painting on large sheets of bark used for the walls of shelters was seen when the Europeans first arrived, and the earliest recorded bark paintings were collected on Essington Island between 1838 and 1878.

Bark is peeled from the trunks of stringybark trees (*Eucalyptus tetradonta*) during the wet season when the sap is rising and the bark is easy to remove. The curved sheet of bark is cured and made pliable, then flattened under weights for a few days while it dries. Next, the rough outer layer is removed and the inner surface rubbed smooth in readiness for painting. The colours used by bark painters in Arnhem Land are a range of red and yellow ochres, white from kaolin or pipeclay, and black which is usually obtained from charcoal or, on Groote Eylandt, from manganese nodules. The sites at which ochres are quarried are often of important ritual and political significance. Colours and the substances from which they are made are symbolic in themselves. White clay is used in mourning, red ochre is associated with the blood of the ancestor-beings who now reside in the earth. For the artist Narritjin Maymuru, the colours expressed the personal nature of his work. White represented his bones, red his blood, yellow his body-fat and black his skin.

A range of brushes is made from a variety of fibres and sticks, the ends of which are either frayed by chewing or have hairs or feathers attached. Broad areas of background colour are often blocked in using the hands. A particularly fine brush made of several long hairs attached to a stick is used to paint intricate cross-hatched patterns. In recent years commercially available brushes have been used, and these are modified to suit the specific needs of the artist.

The traditional fixatives used to bind the pigments include wax, the yolk of birds' eggs, resins and the sap of orchid plants. Since the 1960s, these binding agents have been largely replaced by more readily available and easier to handle synthetic wood-glues. The results generally are similar to those achieved with traditional binders, although some artists prefer to use a more concentrated mixture of glue and pigment to produce a glazed surface on their work. The durable properties of commercial binders make them suitable for the production of art intended for the outside world. Until this became a consideration, the permanence of bark paintings was apparently not important to artists. Paintings made for particular purposes were either destroyed or discarded once their secular or ritual function was fulfilled. As elsewhere in Aboriginal Australia, the process of making art was often more important than the finished product.

Paintings are executed with the bark lying flat, either on the ground or on the artist's lap. As the painting is composed the bark is rotated, and the finished product may have no fixed viewing orientation. As paintings express the relationships between things on social, spiritual and physical planes, the placement of elements in relation to the cardinal points of the compass is often significant. However, the position of dominant images may also indicate a preferred orientation. Narritjin Maymuru's painting *Nyapililngu at Djarrakpi* has 58 both types of reference.

The systems of visual communication in Arnhem Land feature figurative or schematic images and conventional and geometric designs, either separately or more usually in combination. Paintings fall into a number of regional stylistic categories. In West Arnhem Land, bark paintings tend to feature naturalistic images against a plain ground, while the use of geometric designs covering the entire painting surface is more prevalent towards the east. In practice the question of style is more complex than a single regional division would suggest. In Arnhem Land, people distinguish between styles according to a number of related criteria, including the type of country artists occupy – freshwater, saltwater, forest or rocky – and most importantly, the subject of the work and the artists' clan and language-group affiliation. A further influential factor is an artist's moiety affiliation – that is, to which of the two complementary social groups he or she belongs. In much of Arnhem Land the moieties are known as Dhuwa and Yirritja. Moiety membership, inherited patrilineally, determines an artist's rights to use particular designs and patterns.

The use of cross-hatched patterns is a feature of Arnhem Land paintings. The patterns are prescribed designs which identify clans. In the western half of Arnhem Land the cross-hatching is referred to as *rarrk*, while towards the east the patterns are known as *miny'tji* and *dhulang*. The clan designs were handed down by the ancestors and are used in a variety of circumstances, from the making of bark paintings in the public domain to body painting in ceremony. They impart a notion of brightness which signifies the presence of ancestral or spiritual power in a work. Today, artists often elaborate on these designs as they seek to give their paintings vibrancy.

In painting, the major ancestral dramas such as the Wagilag and the Djang'kawu are usually depicted in established compositional structures which include specific iconographic elements arranged in prescribed ways – much as tradition influences the depiction of biblical themes in European art. Here, too, the structures are flexible enough to allow scope for variation, innovation and artistic individuality.

Arnhem Land's range of art styles can be divided broadly by region into four main groups: those of the Kunwinjku and Kuninjku language groups of the west, those of the Rembarrgna and related groups of the centre, the styles of the Yolngu people of the central and north-east regions, and lastly, the disparate styles of the peoples who live in Arnhem Land's environs.

FIGURES OF TRANSFORMATION: WEST ARNHEM LAND

The West Arnhem Land region extends roughly from the East Alligator River which marks the boundary between Kakadu National Park and Arnhem Land, to the Liverpool and Mann Rivers, taking in the Cobourg Peninsula and a number of islands to the north. Among languages, Kunwinjku in the west, around the town of Gunbalanya (formerly Oenpelli), and Kuninjku in the east towards Maningrida are the main dialects spoken in the region. Minor cultural differences distinguish the two groups.

The paintings on the cave and rock walls of the Arnhem escarpment and bark paintings, the most common form of contemporary art in the area, share many pictorial characteristics, and artists in the region today acknowledge a relationship between their work and the rock art. Figurative images predominate in rock art and also appear in bark painting, but non-figurative designs of the type generally restricted to ceremony appear more frequently on barks.

The figures in West Arnhem Land painting are usually set against monochrome backgrounds, which until the 1970s were often a wash of red ochre. In more recent times, white, yellow and occasionally black grounds have been used. The interiors of the drawn images may

12 Unknown artist, *Mimi spearing a kangaroo*, 1912

13 Jimmy Midjaw Midjaw, *Nadulmi in his kangaroo manifestation, as Wubarr leader*, 1950

be divided into sections, and they are highly decorated with designs similar to those painted on to ritual objects and people's bodies in ceremony. The cross-hatched patterns or *rarrk* identify clans and imbue the object on to which they are painted with the power of supernatural beings. In bark painting artists elaborate on these designs and patterns for visual effects and to enhance the notion of ancestral power. As in the rock paintings, the dynamic and x-ray styles of 2, 12 painting are common. *Mimi* spirits are regarded as having taught the ancestors of the present-day Kunwinjku the art of painting. Not regarded as creator beings, *mimi* can be both benevolent and malevolent. They are held responsible for making the earliest rock paintings in the region.

  Mimi spearing a kangaroo, a bark collected by Spencer in Gunbalanya in 1912, has been regarded as an archetypal image of West Arnhem Land paintings. The kangaroo and the hunter are shown in x-ray style: the kangaroo's backbone and internal organs are clearly

27

visible. The kangaroo is drawn much larger than the hunter to emphasize the main subject of the work. Similar paintings appear on the walls of both bark and rock shelters, and their purpose is often didactic, illustrating the parts of the animal's anatomy and the method of slaughtering.

Similar images may be painted to express concepts of deeper significance. The posture of the kangaroo in Jimmy Midjaw Midjaw's *Nadulmi in his kangaroo manifestation, as Wubarr leader* is like that in *Mimi spearing*, but this subject belongs to the religious sphere. The human ancestor Nadulmi is the creator of the Wubarr primary male initiation ceremony. Characteristic of ancestral beings, Nadulmi has the power of transforming his physical shape. Midjaw Midjaw has depicted Nadulmi in x-ray style, but the designs on the kangaroo's body correspond to body paintings used in the Wubarr. To emphasize the connection with ceremony, Nadulmi is shown wearing white crane feathers and with a ritual dilly bag suspended around his neck. The painting expresses the spiritual or inner nature of the subject.

In West Arnhem Land painting, styles spread through the close family groups or communities in which people live. In the 1950s and 1960s Midjaw Midjaw lived on the island of Minjilang, where a number of artists from different backgrounds worked in close proximity and influenced one other. Initially stimulated by collectors and anthropologists, the group included the prolific bark painter Yirawala (1903–76), a great ritual leader with a wealth of religious knowledge which gave him access to the entire range of Kuninjku iconography, from simple secular images of animals through to the images of the great creation stories, and designs for sacred ceremony and magic.

Paintings made for purposes of sorcery (a practice allegedly discontinued following the interventions of missionaries) are found on the rock walls of the region as well as on sheets of bark. They proliferated in the atmosphere of uncertainty on Minjilang, where missionary influence was strong, and where until the 1960s Aboriginal people of 'mixed blood' had been resettled. A significant body of bark paintings was produced in response to the interest in the subject shown by the anthropologists Ronald and Catherine Berndt and the Czech artist, ethnologist and collector Karel Kupka.

Aboriginal people recognize two main forms of magical activity. One is regarded as beneficial and is practised to produce positive results. A painting of a human figure may be intended to encourage

14 Paddy Compass Namatbara,
Maam spirit, c. 1963

affection in another, or an image of a pregnant woman to promote fertility. The other form, sorcery, is undertaken for negative or malevolent purposes and is often employed in relation to offences of a sexual nature, where a jilted lover seeks revenge, for example, or in retribution for a personal slight. Sorcery images have a number of distinguishing features: the figure may be drawn with multiple limbs and distended organs, and the body contorted in unnatural positions. Occasionally limbs and body orifices are shown pierced by sting-ray barbs which are intended to inflict great pain or death on the victim.

In *Maam spirit*, Paddy Compass Namatbara expresses disfigure- 14
ment by adding two legs, and exaggerates the penis to suggest sexual misconduct. *Maam*, a name given to the non-sacred aspect of the soul, is a malevolent entity said to remain with the bones of the dead person, while the sacred aspect of the soul makes the journey to a sacred place in the land of the deceased.

The school of art which developed at Minjilang is replicated today in the family groups who live together on the mainland. The

15 Bobby Barrdjaray Nganjmira, *Kangaroo and crocodile*, 1984

Nganjmiras, a family of Kunwinjku people belonging to the Djalama clan, are some of the most renowned artists. The brothers Peter Nganjmira (1927–87), Jimmy Nakkurridjidjilmi Nganjmira (1917–82) and Bobby Barrdjaray Nganjmira were prolific artists from the 1950s on. Bobby Nganjmira has painted on rock and produced a large
15 body of bark paintings. The work illustrated recalls the hunting scene in the painting collected by Spencer in 1912. A feature of Bobby Nganjmira's work, however, is his elaboration on the patterns of *rarrk*, which influenced a number of younger Kunwinjku artists.

16 In *Yingarna, the Rainbow Serpent*, one of Bobby Nganjmira's protegés, Bruce Nabekeyo, depicts Yingarna as the creator, the First Mother of the Kunwinjku. Nabekeyo has painted Yingarna with waterlilies on its back to indicate its presence in the waterhole which is its home. The Serpent is depicted swallowing people whom it will regurgitate later, in a transformed state, as features of the landscape. The theme of swallowing and regurgitation is commonly used through much of Aboriginal Australia as a metaphor for the transition

16 Bruce Nabekeyo, *Yingarna, the Rainbow Serpent*, 1989, from the series *The story of the yam*

17 Robin Nganjmira, *Likanaya*, 1989

from one metaphysical state of being to another. It is a feature of many ancestral stories concerning the genesis of the world, and it is employed in ceremony to effect the transformation of initiates to a higher spiritual level.

Another artist taught by Bobby Nganjmira, Robin, the son of Jimmy Nganjmira, is typical of a number of painters of his generation in elaborating and inventing patterns of *rarrk* which go beyond the prescribed clan patterns. He uses the device in *Likanaya* to suggest images seen through the surface of water. Likanaya and her sister Marayka are two daughters of Yingarna who escaped the advances of the giant Luma Luma by jumping into a waterhole and growing fish-tails.

Not all Kunwinjku accord Yingarna the role of the original creator. The artist Djawida also belongs to the Djalama clan, but his country, Kudjekbinj, lies away from that of the Nganjmira family, and he paints Nawura as the principal ancestral being. Nawura travelled through the rocky landscape creating sacred sites and giving people the attributes of culture. He taught men how to catch freshwater fish, while his wives taught women how to make food-collecting bags with loops so that they could be carried around their necks, leaving their hands free for wielding digging sticks. As with Yingarna and Ngalyod, Nawura's powers of physical transformation are expressed by the combination of characteristics of different species. In *Nawura, Dreamtime ancestor spirit*, his head has a long pointed snout and curved jaw similar to that of the crocodile depicted to his right. Djawida emphasizes the non-human nature of his figures by giving Nawura and his wives six fingers on each hand. The various species in the painting feature prominently in the Nawura epic.

The art of the Kuninjku in the eastern part of the region also features Yingarna, here called Yinarnga. While Yinarnga is regarded as the all-pervasive principal ancestral being, one of her Rainbow Serpent offspring, Ngalyod, is associated with specific sites.

In Peter Marralwanga's *Ngalyod, the Rainbow Serpent* the Snake is shown at Manabinbala on the Liverpool River, where great tides create a dangerous whirlpool, suggested in the painting by the swirling curve of the figure. In pushing the form of the crocodile-headed serpent to the edges of the bark to create a field of *rarrk*, Marralwanga expresses his dominant concern with spiritual forces. Marralwanga was taught by his uncle Yirawala to paint the *rarrk* designs which were to become the hallmark of his later work. Marralwanga did not begin to produce paintings for sale until he was

17

18

19

19 Peter Marralwanga, *Ngalyod, the Rainbow Serpent*, 1981

20 (*right*) Crusoe Kuningbal, *Mimi spirits*, 1979

over fifty, when his senior position gave him the authority to develop many unorthodox *rarrk* patterns through varying combinations of ochres and angles of lines, to produce areas of unusual colour and stimulating visual effects.

The device of drawing figures to the extremities of the bark is also a feature of the art of John Mawandjul who was profoundly influenced by Marralwanga's paintings. *Rainbow Serpent's antilopine kangaroo* shows a horned Yinarnga giving birth to the Rainbow Serpent Djangkarla in the guise of a kangaroo. Djangkarla's kangaroo head can be seen in the top left-hand corner of the painting, and Yinarnga's to the right. The protrusions on the upper chests of Djangkarla and Yinarnga represent the gullet of emus in which they store the food they will later regurgitate and swallow again. The detail reinforces the concept of transition through the process of swallowing and regurgitation, comparable to the effects of initiation ceremonies.

21

34

21 John Mawandjul, *Rainbow Serpent's antilopine kangaroo*, 1991

22 Mick Kubaku, *Dird*, 1991

The painting is dominated by Mawandjul's sweeping patterns of *rarrk*, which place the subject in the realm of the metaphysical.

In the cosmology of the Kuninjku the moon possessed human form. The Moon ancestor dies, but unlike humans, he is capable of
22 reappearing in the same physical form. Mick Kubaku's *Dird* shows the full moon dying and becoming the crescent of the new moon. The human aspect of Dird is expressed through the depiction of his bones. Typical of Kubaku's work, *Dird* adheres to older, less elaborate styles of *rarrk* in preference to the innovations favoured by many contemporary Kuninjku painters.

There is wide scope for invention in sculpture as well as in painting among Kuninjku artists. Crusoe Kuningbal has created innovative
20 sculptures of *mimi* figures for ceremonial purposes and similar ones for
11 sale. In contrast to the animated painted *mimi* images, Kuningbal's sculpted figures are static. They are painted with a red ground and decorated with rows of white dots. Such figures are used in exchange-ceremonies called Mamurrng, performed to celebrate the birth of a male child, where they watch over the wrapping of carved wooden bones. They are related to *djuandjuan* figures made of paperbark covered in bush string, known from the 1940s, which were used as grave-markers. In the last ten years of his life Kuningbal was a prolific carver of *mimi* figures. Since his death in 1984, the tradition has continued with his son Crusoe Kurddal (born 1964), who often makes figures up to three or four metres high.

SACRED DIGGING STICKS AND DILLY BAGS: CENTRAL ARNHEM LAND

3 The region of Central Arnhem Land, between the Liverpool and Mann Rivers, and the Blyth River towards the town of Ramingining, is occupied by a number of language groups who share ceremonies, customs and beliefs with the Kuninjku. These groups include the Dangbon, Kurrkoni, Gunardba, and Rembarrnga who also possess vast areas of land concentrated in southern Arnhem Land and beyond to Jarruluk. The styles of graphic art in the region mark a transition from the figurative images of the west to the more conventionalized designs and complex compositions found in the east.

That there is no hard and fast division between east and west can be
23, 22 seen from the work of Wally Mandarrk, who like Kubaku maintained the use of traditional techniques in producing bark paintings for sale, including the use of natural fixatives to bind the pigments well after the introduction of synthetic glues. Mandarrk

38

lived in the rock country of the upper reaches of the Tonkinson and Cadell Rivers. His affiliations to the Kune and the Kuninjku on the Liverpool River to the west are evident in his style of painting, illustrating how cultural and artistic influences travel along river systems. The figures in *Narrangem and Naldaluk, Lightning Spirits* are also similar to those found in the rock paintings of the region, and indeed, Mandarrk often painted on rock walls. This painting depicts spirits responsible for creating the spectacular curtains of lightning which accompany the drenching rains of the wet season. Narrangem, on the right, wears at his waist a stone axe to make thunder, while the lines emanating from the figures are streaks of lightning and the circles represent smooth stones made by lightning striking the ground.   23

Ronnie Djambardi's rendering of figures in *Wandurk and his two wives* is similar to Mandarrk's. The figures are shown in full and front-   24

39

25 Les Midikuria, *Digging sticks and sacred dilly bag at Ginajangga*, 1988

26 England Bangala, *Modj (Rainbow Serpent)*, 1988

27 Dorothy Galalebda, *Djinggabardabiya (triangular pandanus skirt)*, 1989

on to the picture plane. The *rarrk* is restricted to clearly defined sections of the torso, in the manner of ritual body painting in a major Kurrkoni ceremony featuring Wandurk for which Djambardi is responsible. Djambardi, however, has used the entire painting surface, in keeping with styles prevalent here and to the east.

In *Modj (Rainbow Serpent)* England Bangala shows the creator-snake as part of the land. The dynamic curve of its body expresses its sheer strength, while simultaneously representing the course of the Cadell River which is its domain. Modj's supernatural powers are contained in the black ceremonial bags around its neck, while eggs, indicative of its procreative energies, appear above the tail on the right. Its home is shown both as the white crescent in the lower half of the painting indicating a rock in the water, and as the white circle at the top left representing a hole on the riverbank.

26

28 Lena Yaringura, *Bok'narru, Rembarrnga male dancing belt*, 1989

At Gochan Jiny-Jirra on the Cadell River, Bangala, a Yirritja man, is the ceremonial leader for a group of families which includes his daughter, the artist Dorothy Galalebda, and her husband Les Midikuria.

Galalebda's apprenticeship as a painter began when she was twenty. Under the guidance of Midikuria, she at first filled in the *rarrk* in his paintings, the usual method of teaching the art of painting, and later learned to paint Midikuria's themes. Recognizing her ability as a painter, Bangala encouraged Galalebda to paint and taught her his stories. As moiety affiliation is patrilineally inherited, Galalebda is Yirritja like her father. Under the marriage rule her husband is Dhuwa, as customarily marriages are made between members of the opposite moieties. Galalebda's experience demonstrates one way in which an artist may gain rights to paint the themes belonging to the opposite moiety.

The main motif in *Djinggabardabiya (triangular pandanus skirt)* is the skirt woven from pandanus-fibres and worn like an apron, symbolic of Gunardba women. In the top right section a meander represents the waterweed *gapalma*, depicted again to either side in the bottom register to illustrate how it can trap unwary people. The waterweed once snared the ancestral Djinggabardabiya skirt at a place which is now the underwater sacred site at Nanganambirri. While the painting is in the genre of her father's work, and indeed he paints this subject often, Galalebda has developed a personal approach enhanced by her distinctive use of *rarrk*.

The fibre arts continue to be one of the major forms of artistic 28, 29 expression for the women of Arnhem Land, although men also weave items for ceremonial and daily use. Artists emphasize the textural qualities of weavings. As in bark painting and sculpture, the scope of fibre objects is continually enhanced through innovation in style and experimentation with new dyes, materials and techniques of weaving. The white cockatoo feathers in Lena Yaringura's *Bok'narru, Rembarrnga male dancing belt* represent a recent introduction among the Rembarrnga. Lena Djamaraku's *Djerrh, bush string carrying bag* incorporates lines of feathered string. The *djerrh* is used by both men and women as a collecting bag or to hold personal possessions, and it can be used in ritual. The various types of string and pandanus-fibre bags, skirts, mats and nets form part of the symbolic imagery used to express the daily and the religious experience.

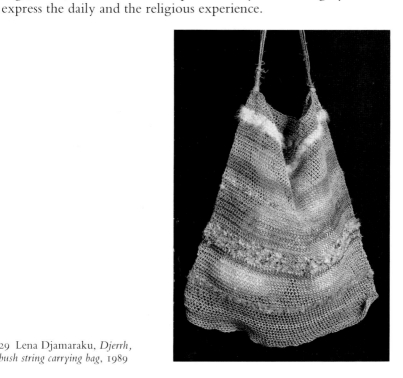

29 Lena Djamaraku, *Djerrh,*
bush string carrying bag, 1989

30 Jack Kala Kala, *Balangu, two sharks*, 1986

31 *(right)* Paddy Fordham Wainburranga, *How World War II began (through the eyes of the Rembarrnga)*, 1990

Objects made of woven fibres play prominent roles in ancestral events. Kunmatj, the sacred dilly bag, was carried by one of the major totemic beings of the Balngnarra clan of the Rembarrnga people, Balangu the Shark. Balangu emerged in eastern Arnhem Land, and his creative exploits link the Murrungun/Djinang and Djambarrpuyngu groups to the Balngnarra. The ancestral Shark (depicted as two sharks in Jack Kala Kala's painting) gave people the humanizing elements of ceremony and law. As Balangu travelled from the east in the wet season, the river-waters rose and he was washed far inland to a waterhole where his spirit resides (at Nangalala on the Glyde River beyond Rembarrnga country). Here Balangu entered the ground, to resurface at other inland lagoons. Red ochre deposits found at these sites were created by Balangu as his body struck the earth.

30

Kunmatj the dilly bag appears as the custodian of the waterhole in *Digging sticks and sacred dilly bag at Ginajangga* by Kala Kala's younger brother (and Galalebda's husband), Les Midikuria, who emerged as an artist after Kala Kala's death in 1987. The painting portrays the ancestral digging sticks named Gungarnin walking through the country and plunging into the earth to create the waterholes which are depicted as circles along the base of the bark. The elements are painted as though they are seen under water, an effect achieved by the innovative combinations of *rarrk* patterns and wide range of colour. Midikuria mixes ochres, charcoal and pipeclay to make pinks, oranges and greens in a manner rare in bark painting.

The diversity of approach to painting among the Rembarrnga is illustrated in the work of Paddy Fordham Wainburranga from Jarruluk in the south, who favours expressionistic and dynamic figurative images and shuns the use of *rarrk*, although he creates a similar luminosity through the use of dots. While much of his work concerns *balangjalngalan* spirits and the ancestral events which resulted in the creation of his country, Wainburranga's work reveals the scope of bark painting to provide Aboriginal perspectives on historical events.

How World War II began (through the eyes of the Rembarrnga) records an event concerning the Japanese pearl divers who used to work the north coast of Australia. The bottom right panel shows an exchange involving Aboriginal women – the Japanese are identified by the

32 Brian Nyinawanga, *Bones*, 1982

short trousers they wear. The lower central panel shows a pearl diver leading a woman to the boats. In 1941 an incident developed between the local people and the Japanese which led to the latter retreating to Darwin, where they were then expelled by government officials (seen in the top right panel, wearing cowboy hats and guns). A few months later, in 1942, Japanese aeroplanes (shown in the left of the painting) bombed the northern coast of Australia. The Rembarrnga, on whom the war was to have far-reaching social effects as many were recruited to work on military installations, felt they had contributed to the start of hostilities.

32 Like Crusoe Kuningbal before him, Brian Nyinawanga, a Rembarrnga artist, developed sculptural types for use in ritual but also for sale. Nyinawanga carves and paints animal and human figures in wood which are then wrapped in paperbark bundles. Often these composite sculptures represent human skeletons; in some cases the bundles are displayed unwrapped and with the contents laid out, or they may be presented wrapped or partially open. *Bones* is made up of three sculpted skeletons; the bones are of a father and his two daughters who were killed for failing to uphold customary marriage-

46

promises. The work relates ancient events and is didactic in nature. Parcels of carved and painted bones are used in Mamurrng exchange ceremonies along with carved *mimi* figures such as those by Kuningbal. The *mimi* watch over the wrapping of the bundle, which is carried throughout the ceremony.

RITES OF PASSAGE OF THE YOLNGU: CENTRAL ARNHEM LAND

A second main cultural group in Central Arnhem Land is made up of the clans whose country lies from Maningrida east to Ramingining 3 and the island of Milingimbi. The clans have ties with the Rembarrnga and related groups but are more closely affiliated to, and share ceremonies and Dreamings with the clans in North East Arnhem Land. The people in this part of Central Arnhem Land and further to the east refer to themselves by the generic term 'Yolngu', meaning 'Aboriginal people'. Here, while clans own land, ceremony, ritual objects and Dreamings, art styles are generally perceived to be associated with the broader language groups and moiety affiliation.

Among the most important Dhuwa moiety themes in Central Arnhem Land is that of Wititj the Great Python and the Wagilag 33-5 Sisters. This chronicles the creative acts of the ancestral sisters as they travelled from south-eastern Arnhem Land, culminating in an epic encounter with Wititj.

The two Wagilag Sisters have children through incestuous relationships with their clansmen, forcing them to leave their inland country and journey north and then west towards the sea. As they travel, they come across animals, plants and country on which they confer names, and by so doing, bring them into being. They make camp at Mirrarrmina waterhole in Liyagalawumirri country, unaware this is the sacred home of Wititj, the Python. Wititj is angered by their presence. Sucking in the waters of the lagoon, he rears erect in the sky and spits to form the rain clouds of the first monsoon season. The Sisters perform songs and dances to avert the deluge and thunderstorm which follow, and take shelter in a bark hut they have made. Wititj suddenly descends and swallows the women, their children and all their belongings. As Wititj raises himself again into the sky, floodwaters cover the earth.

Wititj explains his actions to other ancestral pythons and is made to realize that he has erred in swallowing those who share the same moiety affiliation. The Python sickens and crashes to the ground, leaving the impression of his body in the earth. He vomits out the women and the children, and creates a strong wind which causes the floodwaters to abate. The action of swallowing and vomiting is repeated, but now Wititj regurgitates only the women, who become two large boulders at Mirrarrmina.

The songs and dances performed by the women to stop the rain are revealed to the Wagilag men who had followed. The men are instructed to return home and teach these rites to others to guarantee the continuation of the cycles of nature. Although this is just one aspect of the purpose of the ritual, the Wagilag story emphasizes the importance of religious ceremony, a major function of which is to take an individual from one level of spiritual being to a higher one. The acts of swallowing and regurgitation, as seen in the paintings of Nabekeyo and Mawandjul in West Arnhem Land, once again provide the metaphor for spiritual transformation.

The Wagilag theme presents the opportunity to study the development in a genre of painting over a period of half a century in the work of three artists of an equivalent ritual status, and with a similar level of access to the myriad meanings associated with the subject. The earliest attributable painting of this theme is by Tjam (Sam) Yilkarri Kitani and dates from 1937. In part, the painting is descriptive of the events that occurred at Mirrarrmina. It is composed around the image of Wititj, whose meandering form emerges from the circular waterhole along the bottom edge of the painting to coil around four shapes indicating the Wagilag women and their children, whose footprints are also depicted. The engulfing image of Wititj indicates the process of swallowing, and is the basic structural element which identifies the Wagilag theme in painting. In the upper section the figure of one of the Sisters is seen, upside down in this orientation. The triangular shape seen in the upper right is that made by Wititj's body as it hit the earth. Yilkarri indicates the ritual associations of the event through images which are found in ceremonial ground-sculptures, such as the triangle and the meandering line of the serpent. The composition is divided into two sections, both of which contain images relating to the narrative and to the ritual.

The Wagilag story is the focus of the major Dhuwa ceremonies where deeper levels of religious knowledge are revealed to initiates. The rituals, the Kunapipi in particular, have been of great importance in sustaining traditional beliefs since the advent of Christianity to the region.

When Dawidi Djulwarak inherited his position as leader of the Liyagalawumirri in 1956, he did not have the ritual status to exercise

33 Tjam (Sam) Yilkarri Kitani, *Wagilag*, 1937

34 Dawidi Djulwarak, *Wagilag religious story*, 1965

his responsibilities, and his ceremonial duties were assumed initially
by his uncle Yilkarri and later by Tom Djawa. By 1963, however,
Dawidi was entitled to paint the entire Wagilag repertoire. Many of
the elements of Yilkarri's painting are also recognizable in Dawidi's
Wagilag religious story of 1965. Here again the painting is divided into
two sections, isolating the figuratively depicted narrative and ritual
elements from a conventional depiction of the landscape where the
Wagilag events occurred. In the lower section, the curling form of
Wititj appears again as the dominant image. The upper section is

34

49

35 Paddy Dhatangu, *The Wagilag Sisters story*, 1983

composed of repeated rectangles of cross-hatched designs, the curved shape of the monsoon cloud, lines of dots signifying rain and vertical bands of lightning and thunder, combined to depict the rains of the first monsoon fertilizing the ground. These designs refer to the powers of the ancestral beings invoked, metaphorically drenching the land.

Like Dawidi, Paddy Dhatangu was guided in the art of painting by Yilkarri. In *The Wagilag Sisters story* Dhatangu highlights the flora and fauna described in the narrative, but he has transformed the conventional structure for depicting the Wagilag. Instead of meandering from the waterhole, the coiled shape of the python dominates the picture, and its contours imply the waterhole at Mirrarrmina. The triangular ceremonial ground is omitted, but the formal arrangement of the footprints, the prominence of a cabbage-palm painted with clan designs to the left in the painting and the ritual objects shown to the right, all emphasize the ceremonial aspects of the story.

Comparison of the three artists' treatment of the Wagilag theme yields an insight into the individuality of approach and artistic expression to be seen in bark paintings. While the compositions differ, each work adheres to the pictorial structures which identify the theme.

50

36 Peter Bandjuljul,
*Djang'kawu creator ancestors
and Gachalan the goanna at
Mewirnbi*, 1982

While the Wagilag Sisters' story is associated with the inland freshwater country, one of the other major Dhuwa sagas, the Djang'kawu, belongs to coastal saltwater clans. The Djang'kawu are commonly described as two sisters and their brother who came from the east, giving birth to the clans and creating sacred sites. Peter Bandjuljul's *Djang'kawu creator ancestors and Gachalan the goanna at* 36 *Mewirnbi* is essentially a figurative rendition of events. In the upper section, the Djang'kawu ancestors are shown under a bark shelter. To each side they are depicted carrying their children. Above them is a detail of the conventional ritual design used to identify the Djang'kawu: the cross-like form of rounded shapes representing the freshwater lagoons and the lines joining them indicating the routes the

37 Tom Djawa, *Crabs*, 1969

38 (*right*) David Malangi, *Gunmirringgu*, 1967

Djang'kawu travelled. (This design is elaborated in a painting by
45 Daypurryun.) Bandjuljul also illustrates the connection between the
Djang'kawu and another ancestral being, Gachalan the goanna,
where the paths of the two Dreamings cross at Mewirnbi. The
goannas are depicted surrounding a hollow log in the lower register of
the painting. The circular shape in the middle of the painting
represents the waterhole at Mewirnbi.

Details of the creation stories are painted with particular reference
37 to the locality in which events occurred. Tom Djawa's *Crabs*, for
3 instance, depicts a site in Liyagawumirri country opposite Galiwinku
(Elcho Island) where the Djang'kawu created fish and crabs in the
mangrove swamps. The artist, a senior Yirritja moiety man, had the
right to paint Dhuwa Djang'kawu images through his matrilineally
inherited connection with this Dreaming.

The Djang'kawu ancestors are also among the personal totems of
38 David Malangi, but his predominant subjects derive from the story of

Gunmirringgu, the Great Hunter, at Ngurrunguwa, a site in Malangi's country. The saga of Gunmirringgu concerns death, mortuary rituals and beliefs about the soul.

The Great Hunter camped under a white berry tree and began to cook a kangaroo he had killed when a poisonous King Brown snake bit him, causing his death. *Gunmirringgu* shows the Hunter's body decorated with clan designs and surrounded by ritual dancers in the centre left of the painting. The ceremony involves the killing and eating of kangaroos, an act which refers to the death of a person, while the dissection of the carcass symbolizes the exhumation of human bones in readiness for the reburial ceremony when the bones are placed in a hollow-log coffin (p. 74). According to the Manharrngu, the pelican shown in the tree guides the soul to the land of the dead. The flowering stringybark tree in the upper register of the painting is analogous with the Morning Star pole to which are attached the several morning stars, symbolized by the white berries.

For the Dhuwa moiety the morning star is an important element in post-funeral ceremonies. The religious stories and ritual associated with the morning star are, like the Wagilag story, symbolic of the passage of the soul from one state of being to another – in this case, from the inner spirit world prior to birth, through the physical phase of life, and at death to the land of dead. On one level the Morning Star story relates the transition from night to day. The spirits of the dead keep the Banumbirr, the Morning Star, in a dilly bag and send it out into the night sky. The Star is attached to a long string, by which it is retrieved and returned to its bag as the sun rises.

Banumbirr the Morning Star by Jack Wunuwun is layered with metaphorical allusions to the cycle of life and symbolic references to the natural world. In the central panel, the onset of the monsoon rains which fertilize the earth is suggested by a flock of ibis. Below, the ceremonial Morning Star poles are symbolic of procreation. The form of the poles, where the large feathered fans on top and attached to the strings represent the Morning Star, is repeated in the right-hand panel in the forms of the tubers of the yam plant. The yam flowers during Mayaltha, from January to March late in the wet season, the period of growth. In the season of Midawar, at the end of the wet period, the swollen rivers carry great numbers of fish which are caught in traps, as depicted in the panel on the left. The fish-trap is symbolic of a container of souls. The complex relationships between different realms of experience are succinctly expressed in this painting.

During the second half of the dry period, in Rrarrandhar (August

39 Don Gundinga, *Honey Dreaming at Walkumbimirri*, 1984

40 Jimmy Wululu,
*Niwuda, Yirritja native
honey*, 1986

41 George Milpurrurru,
Fire and Water Dreaming,
1989

to September), wild bees' nests full of honey are common. The treatment of the subject of honey in art illustrates the relationship between moiety affiliation and graphic representation. Yolngu (as the Aboriginal peoples of the region refer to themselves) identify four types of honey, the main ones being *yarrpany* which belongs to the Dhuwa moiety, and *niwuda* which is Yirritja. *Yarrpany* is usually depicted in a figurative and relatively naturalistic manner. Don Gundinga's *Honey Dreaming at Walkumbimirri* is densely packed with images – human and spirit figures, ceremonial objects, animals and insects, tools, collecting bags and drops of honey. The surface is highly animated with different coloured outlines, the bustling juxtaposition of images and the play of areas of cross-hatching which belie the images they decorate. The dynamic nature of the image conveys the presence of the animating spirit of the Honey Ancestor in the land.

In contrast, *Niwuda, Yirritja native honey* by Jimmy Wululu is an elaboration on the conventional method of representing Yirritja

56

honey in painting. The diamond pattern indicates full and empty cells, while the dots represent the bees and pollen-balls of the host tree. The powers of the Honey Spirit are evoked by this pattern, which is also painted on to the chests of participants in the related ceremony, and on the bodies of the deceased members of the Yirritja moiety who are connected to the Honey Ancestor.

One of the most prolific Yirritja painters of the contemporary era is George Milpurrurru. Milpurrurru possesses a range of subjects 41 commensurate with his high ritual standing as a ceremonial leader of the Ganalbingu, and his paintings are characterized by vibrant surfaces enhanced by the serial repetition of motifs. In *Fire and Water Dreaming*, sets of ritual emblems are formally arranged in two sections of the painting, while the upper register depicts a river. Milpurrurru uses intricate cross-hatched clan patterns to create an optical shimmer which suggests the forces of the ancestral Fire and Water Dreamings that imbue his country at Ngalyindi.

The concept of painting the land held by Yolngu artists is that it establishes an individual's or group's relationship to the country. In 42

42 Clara Wubugwubuk, *Walmi grass – munyigani edible tuber*, 1990

43 Johnny Bulun Bulun, *Sacred waterholes surrounded by totemic animals of the artist's clan*, 1981

Walmi grass – munyigani edible tuber Clara Wubugwubuk, one of a number of women who are making their mark as bark painters around Ramingining, depicts a landscape of running water and grass. The edible tuber depicted in the lower section of the painting is the artist's personal totem, and serves to reaffirm her link with the country and the rights and responsibilities she enjoys. 42

Freshwater lagoons are considered by the Yolngu to be the repositories of the souls of the unborn, and the places to which the souls of the dead will return. The pivotal role of the waterhole is evident in the composition of *Sacred waterholes surrounded by totemic animals of the artist's clan* by Johnny Bulun Bulun. Bulun Bulun makes the circular clan-wells the foci of the composition. Among the surrounding images of flora and fauna are magpie-geese, the major totem of the Gurrumba Gurrumba, the artist's clan. Characteristically for Central Arnhem Land paintings, the compositional structure of Bulun Bulun's bark reinforces the thematic content of the work. 43

ANCESTRAL MAPS OF THE YOLNGU: NORTH EAST ARNHEM LAND

In North East Arnhem Land, from the island of Galiwinku to Yirrkala and south along the coast, the influence of clan membership is paramount. In painting, the underlying compositional structures, or templates, identify each clan and act as a conceptualized map of the clan's land. The structures encode sets of relationships between people, their country and ancestral beings. The emphasis here is on formal designs and prescribed compositions. As the market for Aboriginal art began to flourish in the 1960s, artists became concerned that some of the purely conventionalized designs, as painted on to objects in ceremony, were too sacred in nature to be seen by outsiders. Since each geometric design carries many layers of meaning, and there is a range of figurative versions to represent each of these, artists were able to de-sanctify paintings by introducing figurative images. In this way paintings retain deeper meanings to the Yolngu themselves but are made suitable for public display.

A fundamental concern among artists in North East Arnhem Land is to take paintings from a rough, dull state to one of brightness and brilliance. This is achieved through the visual density of the *dhulang* or cross-hatched clan designs, and the build-up of layers of colour culminating in the use of white cross-hatching. The effect aimed for is one of visual shimmer, which accords with concepts of painting in the ceremonial context. In ritual, paintings on bodies, sculptures, coffins 58 and objects are not intended to be static images requiring studied contemplation. Rather, since designs embody the power of the supernatural beings, they are intended to be sensed more than viewed. The patterns of *dhulang* are derived from ancestral events: for example, a diamond pattern was burned into the back of the ancestral crocodile while the waves of the sea left patterns on the body of another ancestor.

Among the major Dhuwa themes in the art of North East Arnhem Land are the Djang'kawu ancestors. As with the naturalistic and conventional forms for rendering episodes of the Wagilag story (called Wagilak or Wawilak in North East Arnhem Land) depictions of this theme take on various pictorial forms.

44–5

The Djang'kawu Brother and Sisters encountered various creatures on their voyage to Yalangbara on the eastern shore of Arnhem Land, where they made their first camp. They carried with them dilly bags elaborately decorated with feathers, conical mats, and large digging sticks, all of which were to have important roles in their creative actions. As they travelled west across the land the Djang'kawu named and created all manner of natural species. At every place they camped they made bodies of freshwater by driving their digging sticks into the ground. The sticks themselves became trees. The Sisters would crouch under the pandanus mats and give birth to sacred objects, and to the ancestors of the clans who would inhabit that country.

44

In the upper panel of *The birth of the Djang'kawu children at Yalangbara* by Wandjuk Marika the Djang'kawu Brother is depicted with a dilly bag around his neck and holding two large digging sticks. To either side is the transformation of the digging stick into a casuarina tree. The central panel shows, in schematic form, the two Djang'kawu Sisters giving birth to the clans. The Rirratjingu clan design which forms the ground of the painting also reads as the pattern of shifting sands on the beach at Yalangbara. The subject of the lower panel is identical but here the event is rendered symbolically. The dotted forms represent the afterbirths, and the clans to which the Sisters gave birth are represented as the six round shapes of the conical mats of the Djang'kawu.

45

The conventional Djang'kawu pattern is shown in Mick Daypurryun's *Sacred waterholes – the Djang'kawu*. The Djang'kawu's digging sticks and dilly bags along with jellyfish are shown in the lower half of the painting. The painting relates to the Djang'kawu in Liyagawumirri land on Galiwinku. The regularity of the design suggests the ordered nature of the creation of the land.

44 Wandjuk Marika, *The birth of the Djang'kawu children at Yalangbara*, 1982

45 Mick Daypurryun, *Sacred waterholes – the Djang'kawu*, 1988

46 Mandjuwi with Kallie Yalkarrawuy, *The Morning Star ceremony*, 1979, installation

A similar grid-structure is found in Mandjuwi's paintings of *The*   46
Morning Star ceremony, a series of works which defines the connection
between the Djang'kawu and Wuluyma, the Yam ancestor and
founder of the Galpu clan's Morning Star ceremony at Galiwinku.
The combination of bark paintings, feathered poles and a sculpture of
Wuluyma in the installation reflects the elaborate interaction between
painted images and three-dimensional forms in ritual circumstances.

47 Mawalan Marika, *Turtle Dreaming*,
c. 1963

48 (*right*) Banduk Marika, *Minyapa ga
Dhanggatjiya*, 1990

The connection between the two ancestral figures of the Rirratj-ingu clan, Mururruma the great turtle-hunter and Djambuwal the Thunderman, is referred to in *Turtle Dreaming* by Mawalan Marika, a noted artist, statesman and ritual leader of the Dhuwa at Yirrkala. Against a ground-pattern of the Rirratjingu clan design representing the sea, seaweed and sand dunes, the long pointed shapes indicate the spouts of water the Thunderman sends down in the monsoon season, while the central image is a waterhole on Dhambaliya (Bremer Island), where the rocks contain Mururruma's spirit.   47

Recognition of women bark painters in Arnhem Land came in the early 1970s when those who had assisted their fathers began to make their own paintings. Among the women artists are Banygul (born 1927) and Dhuwarrwarr Marika (born 1949), who were taught to paint by their father Mawalan. Banygul's younger sister Banduk Marika, however, has pursued printmaking rather than painting. Her linocuts and screenprints adhere to the pictorial traditions of her clan, the Rirratjingu. The techniques involved in cutting linoleum are similar to those used in the layered application of *dhulang* in bark painting and the incision of designs on wood sculptures in North East Arnhem Land. Banduk's linocut *Minyapa ga Dhanggatjiya* shows   48 Mururruma's sons Minyapa and Dhanggatjiya, who were also famous turtle-hunters. A modified version of the Rirratjingu clan design shows the sea with dotted bands to represent sea-urchins and the light glancing off the surface of the water.

Banduk's free-flowing composition contrasts sharply with the highly formal treatment of a ceremonial subject by her father's brother Mathaman Marika. *Wagilak ceremony* depicts a rite performed at the lagoon at Mirrarrmina. The composition of the painting is a conceptualized map of the Arafura lagoon and also a depiction of the formal arrangements of the ceremony. The descendants of the Wagilak are shown below the waters of the lagoon at the centre of the painting. The image synthesizes the creation story of the Wagilak, the rituals they initiated, and the enactment of the ceremonies through time to the present. Mathaman's composition varies considerably from the spiralling structure found in Central Arnhem Land paintings of this theme.

The Honey Ancestor of the Marrakulu clan, Wuyal, is associated with the Wagilak Sisters. Dundiwuy Wanambi's *Wuyal creation story with Gundimulk ceremonial ground* shows Wuyal and a companion who like the Wagilak Sisters travelled from the south. The two ancestors carry spears and axes to extract honey from the bees' nests they find in trees. The hollow tree-trunk has a number of interpretations. Where it falls, it forms both a ceremonial ground and the Gurka'wuy River at Trial Bay, the artist's homeland. The tree is also the ceremonial hollow log shown in the upper register of the painting, where two goannas carry shellfish in their mouths to indicate their association with the sea. As Wuyal chopped the tree, honey flowed into the ground, a metaphor for Wuyal imbuing the earth with his spirit. Dundiwuy's painting reflects some of the processes by which ancestral beings shape the landscape and leave their power in the earth to be tapped by human beings on ceremonial occasions.

Among the ancestral figures of the Yirritja moiety in North East Arnhem Land, Barama and Lany'tjung stand out. There are several versions of the exploits of these ancestors. One describes how Barama emerged from a waterhole in Dhalwangu clan country decorated with clan designs and feathered strings. He floated down the Koolatong River on a log which became embedded in the riverbed at Gangan. From here, he sent Lany'tjung on a mission to distribute the laws, songs, dances, paintings and sacred emblems among the clans. In this way, each clan would have its specific attributes yet all the clans would be affiliated. In the sculpture by Badangga and Waninyambi, Lany'tjung (referred to as Djirrban) is represented with his body covered in the designs he distributed to the various Yirritja clans. The figure is characteristic of North East Arnhem Land sculpture in its post-like features, a form thought to have been introduced by the

49 Mathaman Marika, *Wagilak ceremony*, 1963

50 Dundiwuy Wanambi, *Wuyal creation story with Gundimulk ceremonial ground*, 1990

51 Badangga and Waninyambi, *Djirrban* (Lany'tjung), 1960

52 Birrikidji Gumana, *Lany'tjung story – the death of Lany'tjung*, 1960s

53 Yanggarriny
Wunungmurra, *Minhala the
Long-Necked Tortoise on the
sacred log*, 1990

54 Munggarrawuy Yunupingu,
Lany'tjung story number two,
1959

51 Macassans (p. 21). The white face of Djirrban represents sea-foam, while the long vertical descending from his chin is a Macassan beard, another legacy of the trepang fishermen's influence.

Lany'tjung went north towards Yirrkala and then west towards Milingimbi, however he broke the law by openly displaying the secret objects, an act which brought about his death. The event is
52 commemorated in Lany'tjung story – the death of Lany'tjung by Birrikidji Gumana who was the ceremonial leader of the Yirritja moiety and an influential artist. The focal image of the painting is the figure of Lany'tjung in an elliptical hollow-log coffin during a ritual intended to restore him to life. Birrikidji's variations on the Dhalwangu clan pattern impart a sense of the ebb and flow of spiritual forces. The regular diamond pattern refers to flowing freshwater. In the section above the horizontal fish-trap to the left, the pattern of diamonds running vertically is interrupted by an elliptical shape, indicating freshwater streams running down from the hills into lagoons and out again. The pattern near the tortoise is its wake as it swims by the fish-trap, and the dots represent air-bubbles escaping from its nostrils.

The freshwater tortoise Minhala was one of the creatures created by
53 Barama. Yanggarriny Wunungmurra's sculpture is a rare rendition in three dimensions of Minhala on the sacred log at Gangan. The patterns of flowing water on the outer surfaces of the sculpture wrap around the painted white clay inner surfaces of the log and Minhala's belly. The white clay is synonymous with Minhala's home.

Fire was created by the Crocodile Man, Baru, during a ceremony in Madarrpa clan country. The ancestral fire spread to the land of other clans in the region, thereby providing ritual links between them.
54 Munggarrawuy Yunupingu's Lany'tjung story number two is a compendium of aspects of the Fire Dreaming as it relates to the Gumatj clan. Here, the clan pattern represents sand, while the hatched lines separating the panels indicate submerged sandbanks. In the top-right panel Baru rests at the mouth of the river, while in the panel below he has had the fire design burnt into his skin and his left foreleg incinerated. The lower-left panel depicts the bandicoot who escaped the fire by hiding in a hollow log. Within the cone-shaped dancing ground seen in the bottom-right panel a ceremony is depicted, where the actions of the ancestral beings are performed in the dances of Bandicoot, Wild Honey, Water and Fire. A new Dreaming is called out and danced; this is Dugong, the Sea Cow, represented by the panels of larger diamonds to the upper left.

55 Mutitjpuy Mununggurr, *Dugong hunt*, 1967

56 (*right*) Wakuthi Marawili, *Fire Dreaming with Dugong hunting story*, 1982

57 Liwukang Bukurlatjpi, *Mamu spirit boat*, 1982

The Dugong Dreaming indicates that the ancestral fire spread out to sea, and that the rights of coastal clans to land extend to defined areas offshore. Mutitjpuy Mununggurr's *Dugong hunt* depicts the fire story as it relates to a part of the Madarrpa clan estate off Yathikpa on Blue Mud Bay. Yathikpa is the Dreaming place of the Dugong. The lower-right section depicts two ancestral figures making a harpoon and paddle in preparation for the Dugong hunt. To the left of this scene, the two men are shown in a canoe chasing the Dugong. The Dugong, however, swam away and dived underwater to create the Fire Dreaming site. The harpoon became a ritual object, while the ancestors' canoe became a rock on the shore. The marine environment is further suggested by the fish and flowers of sea-grass upon which Dugong feed. Wakuthi Marawili's *Fire Dreaming with Dugong hunting story* is a geometrically rendered version of the same events.

The Macassans' marked influence on the peoples of coastal Arnhem Land went beyond the introduction of aspects of technology such as metal tools, to influences on art forms, language and symbolism. The subject of *Mamu spirit boat* by the Warramiri artist Liwukang Bukurlatjpi is based on a dream recounted to him by a relative, who saw the spirit of his newborn son in a boat coming from Galiwinku to the mainland. The boat is defined by the central rectangle bounded at all four corners by circles, and its oars appear as the adjacent waisted shapes. The central circle represents the spirit of the boy. In the dream, the boat had eyes like car-headlamps which lit up the way. The circles represent the lamps and the horizontal lines indicate the beams of light. The boat, however, is simultaneously the ancestral Squid, shown twice, head to head; the circles are its eyes and the horizontals reaching to the sides of the bark its tentacles.

This work illustrates how ideas in different realms of experience can be synthesized in painting. The painting has further references. The boat with eyes is one of a number of metaphors for the constellation of the Pleiades, indicating seasonal change in relation to the comings and goings of the Macassans. The Macassan *prahu* (vessel) sailing off towards the horizon symbolizes the journey of the soul of the deceased to the land of the dead.

The journey of the soul is the subject of Luma Luma Yunupingu's *The spirit's journey*, which interprets the transformations the body and soul undergo through the mortuary rituals practised in Arnhem Land. Two stages of the burial take place. The first occurs upon death when the body of the deceased is ritually painted with clan designs and either placed on a platform in a tree or buried. The body is depicted on

55

56

51
57

59

72

a platform in the upper section of the painting. The white cockatoo or *ngerk*, above, will guide the soul to the land of the dead. The lower section of the painting depicts the reburial rite or hollow-log ceremony. For this, the bones are gathered, painted with red ochre, crushed and placed in a prepared hollow-log coffin, previously painted with the relevant clan designs and totemic images. Participants in the ritual erect the hollow-log coffin on the deceased's clan estate, and it is left to the elements. The ceremony marks the safe transition of the soul of the deceased to the land of the dead. Prohibitions, including speech and food taboos, brought into force for kin at the time of death, are now lifted.

59   The sculptures represent, as it were, a cross-section of the coffin, showing the body painted with *dhulang*, the states of decay of the flesh, the skeleton, and the spirit of the deceased. The sculptures are notable for the use of negative space and the placement within it of carved forms. The introduction of specialized woodcarving tools in the early 1980s has permitted the production of more detailed and
51   complex sculptures than were possible at the time *Djirrban* was made, in 1960.

The funerary ceremonies of the Manggalili clan to the south were instituted by the Nyapililngu beings to grieve for their dead brother,
58   the koel-cuckoo Guwak. *Nyapililngu at Djarrakpi* by Narritjin Maymuru symbolically connects the creation of the sand dunes at Djarrakpi to the Manggalili mortuary rituals. The painting is oriented from south, at the top, to north. The two Nyapililngu are constructed from the symbols of women's life. Their bodies are made from digging sticks, dilly bags form their heads, and their faces feature crosses indicating women's breast-girdles. The casuarina trees that form the tops of the women's heads are the final resting-place of Guwak. Ellipses of the lower sections of the women's bodies correspond to both the earth-sculpture the women made for the funeral of their brother and the lake at Djarrakpi.

Along the right edge of the bark, Guwak appears as a length of the possum-fur string that he collected and the women spun to make a sand-ridge that is now the men's side of Djarrakpi. The middle of the painting depicts the lake at Djarrakpi. The Nyapililngu and the line of triangular shapes to the left indicate the sand dunes, the seaward and women's side of the lake. The anvil-shape at the top of the painting represents the casuarina tree which stands at the head of the lake. Like the anvil-shape in the lower section of the painting, it also symbolizes the high cumulus clouds created by the smoke from the fire the

74

59 Luma Luma Yunupingu, *The spirit's journey*, 1984

60 George Jawaranga Wurramara, *Yinikarrka (the Wind Spirit)*, 1984

61 Ginger Riley Munduwalawala, *My country*, 1988

Nyapililngu lit as they mourned their brother. The composition of the painting corresponds to the spatial organization of the burial ceremony and is a map of the country.

Characteristically for Yolngu painting, *Nyapililngu at Djarrakpi* is a matrix of visual puns. Meaning is elaborated and enriched through the multiple references of symbols and their juxtaposition within the work.

58

NARRATIVES ON BARK: GROOTE EYLANDT

Groote Eylandt lies less than fifty kilometres off the coast of North East Arnhem Land in the Gulf of Carpentaria, and is the largest island in an archipelago that includes Bickerton and Chasm Islands. The people of western Groote Eylandt share many of the religious beliefs of those on the mainland, but the pictorial styles of Groote Eylandt art as a whole are markedly distinctive, and are closely related to the rock paintings which abound on the islands. Figures are either simply drawn in silhouette, or else have decorative interior designs

3

62, 60

77

of hatching and cross-hatching, grids, and broken or dotted lines which may refer to body-painting designs or describe terrain or topographical features.

The subjects of bark paintings include ancestral beings and spirits, in both human and animal forms, flora and fauna, the constellations, the three main winds, the Macassans, ceremonies and historic events. Bark paintings are made largely for didactic purposes and as commentaries on events. The earliest barks to be collected from Groote Eylandt date back to 1922, the year after a mission was established there. In the intervening period the styles of painting remained fairly constant, reflecting the relative isolation of the islands. In the 1920s and 1930s, images were loosely composed on unpainted or red backgrounds. In the following two decades black grounds became more common, with figures outlined in red ochre. The black is derived from locally occurring manganese.

Typical of these paintings are the sets of narrative barks produced in the mid-1950s by Thomas Nandjiwarra (1923–89) and Bill Namiayangwa, both concerned with Dreaming episodes and historic events such as battles between rival groups, themes also found in the rock art. Each series is composed to read from right to left. In most cases each bark depicts one moment within an episode, but the detail from the set of seven paintings *An attack by war canoes* by Namiayangwa depicts a temporal sequence. The subject is an attack by Bickerton Island men on Groote Eylandt, where they surprise a man and his five wives. The man is a brave and illustrious fighter who manages to escape to fetch his spears and spear-thrower, with which he puts the attackers to flight and saves his wives. Namiayangwa combines a planar view of the terrain with the figures in profile to show the various events of the episode in one image. The women and the fighter are depicted enclosed by a loop, a device used to indicate both an avenue of escape for the fighter and the route of his return. The figures of the Bickerton men are distributed around the loop, approaching from the lower right and fleeing in the upper left.

Among the more common themes of Groote Eylandt painting are the constellations. The Milky Way is regarded as a river in the sky, full of fish and edible species from which the celestial beings gather their food. Minimini Mamarika depicts the constellations known to Europeans as Orion and the Pleiades. Orion is a man or several men called Burumburumrunya, depicted as three circles across the bar of the T-shape, Orion's belt. The vertical is Orion's sword and it includes, from the bottom up, three fish the men caught and the fire in

62 Bill Namiayangwa, *They surround a man and his five wives, but he escapes*, c. 1955

63 Minimini Mamarika, *Orion and the Pleiades*, 1948

64 Attributed to Nandabitta, *Macassan prahu and trepang curing*, c. 1974

65 Marruwani, *The death of Purukuparli*, 1954 (see p. 85)

which they cooked them. The wives of Burumburumrunya are shown as small circles within the larger round form which represents a grass hut, now to be found in the constellation of the Pleiades.

The totemic winds are a recurring subject of Groote painting. Mamarika, the south-east wind, blows in the first half of the dry season and heralds the departure of the Macassan trepangers from the shores. Designs representing the main winds are said to have been derived from the shape of the sails on Macassan *prahu*, although they are equally likely to be based on rock and waterhole formations. The sail-shape seen in *Macassan prahu and trepang curing*, attributed to Nandabitta, is said by some to represent Mamarika. The painting shows the *prahu* with its crew on board, while people are shown boiling, drying and sorting the sea-cucumber.   64

The opening of manganese mines on Groote Eylandt in 1963 resulted in significant numbers of non-Aboriginal people taking up residence on the island for the first time. This ready market stimulated the production of art and artefacts, and saw a shift in the style of bark painting. The backgrounds of paintings began to be covered with designs, the compositions became more complex, and in some cases, monochrome figures were painted to stand out clearly against these highly decorated backgrounds. The new market's desire for seemingly more sophisticated, or at least more intricate paintings may have provided the impetus for these elaborations.

Yinikarrka (the Wind Spirit) by George Jawaranga Wurramara   60
displays the features of the more recent painting from Groote. Yinikarrka is the ancestral Kestrel who, in human form, camped with his wife and children on the west coast of Bickerton Island. He encountered the Rainbow Serpent Alja who had created the watercourse on Bickerton. Yinikarrka and his family went from camp to camp, leaving waterholes and other permanent signs of their presence. Eventually they turned into birds and made their way to the east coast of Groote where their nests are still to be seen as three caves in a cliff-face.

In the upper section of the painting Yinikarrka is shown as a man standing on rocks searching for members of the artist's clan, the Wurramara, who are swimming in a lagoon on Bickerton Island. The waterhole is depicted as the horizontal band at the centre of the painting. Beside Yinikarrka are the rain clouds which produced the lagoon, their billowing shape resembling a wind-symbol. The formal composition and the profusion of decorative patterns and cross-hatching in the painting show Jawaranga's concern to produce a

81

vibrant picture-surface, similar in effect to paintings in North East Arnhem Land.

Despite their location around the south-eastern part of Arnhem Land in proximity to major bark painting areas to the north and on Groote Eylandt, since 1984 the artists who now live along the Roper River and in the town of Ngukurr have favoured the use of synthetic paints and canvas. A number of the pictorial devices prevalent in northern Arnhem Land paintings are evident at Ngukurr: the imagery is largely figurative, and techniques of hatching and x-ray are used. In *Fish and birds in the shallows*, for example, Wilfred Nalandarra uses a restricted palette but builds visual texture in the bodies of the animals by overlaying lines and dashes of colour. He also indicates the backbone of the creatures in the manner of West Arnhem Land painting.

19, 43

66

Willie Gudipi, one of the instigators of the movement towards art for the outside world, focuses on initiation and mortuary ceremonies in his work. As in *Untitled* he uses a composition of sections within which the action takes place, much as do the Yolngu bark painters. The divisions in Gudipi's paintings isolate parts of the narrative, and also indicate the boundaries of clan estates. The images include

67

66 Wilfred Nalandarra, *Fish and birds in the shallows*, 1989

67 Willie Gudipi, *Untitled*, 1990

68 (*below*) Amy Johnson Jirwulurr, *Some animals have secret songs*, 1990

ancestors in human and animal form, weapons, tools and a plethora of flora which are used to create rich and lively surfaces.

The compositions of Ngukurr paintings are not always so formally 68 structured, however. Amy Johnson Jirwulurr's *Some animals have secret songs* depicts brolgas· (cranes) catching fish. The 'animals' represent the forms adopted by her clan's human ancestors who are seeking places to perform initiation and mortuary ceremonies.

61 *My country* by Ginger Riley Munduwalawala also features a compendium of the ancestral beings who created his clan's, the Mara's, country which lies around Limmen Bight, beyond Arnhem Land on the Gulf of Carpentaria. The serpent in the painting is Bandian, who possesses great powers of transformation. Bandian often appears as two snakes, called Garimala or Kurra Murra, who in turn adopt the identity of another Rainbow Serpent, Wawalu. Yet another manifestation is as the fire-breathing sea-monster Bulukbun who kills people, a reference to the massacres by the first Europeans who came to the region by sea in the late nineteenth century.

The bust-like image of a bird depicted in the lower-right section of *My country* is Ngak Ngak, the sea-eagle who created Yumunkuni Island in the mouth of the Limmen Bight River. In the body of Riley's work, Ngak Ngak is omnipresent, observing the creative dramas that unfold in the Dreaming, an allegory, perhaps, for the artist bearing witness through the eyes of his avian totem to the events that are depicted in the canvases. Riley's paintings also feature rectangular message-sticks or boards which announce initiation and circumcision rites, or invite people to his country. The message-sticks are flanked by two snakes, as at the left in this painting, or by a human figure, as on the right. The meandering forms of the snakes and the use of dots 92 to define contours are pictorial devices also common in the art of the desert, further south.

ART IN ISOLATION: THE TIWI

3 The Tiwi people live on Bathurst and Melville Islands to the north of Darwin. The treacherous channel that separates the islands from the mainland has until this century precluded any meaningful contact with outsiders. Sustained outside influence on Tiwi life commenced when buffalo shooters set up a camp on Melville Island in 1900. Buffalo on the islands were a legacy of the short-lived attempt by the English to establish a settlement in 1824. A more permanent influence has been the Catholic mission which was established at Nguiu on

Bathurst Island in 1911. The result of isolation is evident in several cultural differences between the Tiwi and the mainlanders, and in the development of a number of unique art forms, particularly in sculpture. Ceremonies revolve around two major cycles: the Kulama 69 initiation ritual which celebrates life, and the mortuary rites of the Pukumani. Matrilineal inheritance is an important aspect of Tiwi social structure, and women play a prominent role in most forms of cultural expression, from ceremony to the arts.

In their Dreamings the Tiwi describe a period of genesis in which the ancestors appeared and created social structures, religious laws and the features of the land. The period begins with the emergence of an old blind woman, Mudungkala, who rose out of the ground at Murupianga in south-eastern Melville Island. She crawled across the shapeless earth creating sites and waterways. As she went she carried her three children: two daughters, Wuriupranala and Murupiang-kala, and a son, Purukuparli. Their descendants settled throughout the islands. At the end of the first part of this creation period, Mudungkala departed while her children remained.

At Yipanari, on the eastern tip of Melville Island, Purukuparli married Bima, the great-granddaughter of his sister Murupiangkala. They had a son Jinani, of whom Purukuparli was exceptionally fond. Purukuparli's younger brother Tapara came to their camp and seduced Bima. As a result Jinani was neglected and died. Purukuparli was enraged by the death of his son. Tapara asked his permission to try to bring Jinani back to life, but a fight with Purukuparli ensued. Purukuparli wrapped his son's body in paperbark and carried it out into the sea off Yipanari, decreeing that death would become the fate of all Tiwi. Where Purukuparli drowned, a strong whirlpool formed. Tapara became the moon, and in this form, did not escape Purukuparli's decree, but died only to be reborn.

In *The death of Purukuparli* by Marruwani the final drama of 65 Purukuparli's life is depicted in an iconic manner, with the composition echoing the mounting tension of the narrative. The crescent-shape at the bottom of the painting is Tapara holding the throwing sticks which he used in the fight with Purukuparli. The white crescent above indicates Tapara asking for Jinani's body, which is represented by the horizontal bar at the centre of the painting. The two short white verticals in the dominant shape are Purukuparli's arms holding his dead son; above are his footprints as he walks out into the water. Purukuparli himself is indicated by the yellow half-circle within the round red whirlpool at the top of the painting.

Bima's father, Tokwampini the Honey Bird Man, organized the first Pukumani ceremony for Purukuparli, and directed the making of grave-poles, bark baskets, ceremonial spears and other paraphernalia of traditional Tiwi art. When the ceremony was performed, Tokwampini instructed all the ancestors in the laws of marriage and social behaviour, whereupon they dispersed to metamorphose into the various forms of flora, fauna, heavenly bodies and ritual objects by which they are now known. This ended the creation period.

More than a burial ceremony, Pukumani describes an extraordinary state of being which affects all those connected with the deceased. It includes prohibitions concerning the interaction of certain categories of kin and the touching of particular objects and food, and demands a particular style of behaviour to be followed by the mourners in daily life. Pukumani is lifted when the long sequence of ritual is ended.

69 Laurie Nelson Tuki-al-ila, Bob One Gala-ding-wama, Big Jack Yarunga, Don Burak-madjua, Charlie Quiet Kwangdini and one unknown artist, *Pukumani poles*, 1958

70 Bama Yu (Polly Miller), *Jimwalini, Pukumani basket*, 1984

71 Unknown artist, *Pamijini mourning band*, pre-1912

The ceremony of Pukumani yields much of the art of the Tiwi. Spectacularly painted poles called *tutini* are carved from dense ironwood and used as grave-markers. The Tiwi see the poles as analogous to the human form, for they are intended to represent aspects or associations of the deceased whose grave they surround. Any number of poles may surround a grave, although usually more than twenty signify that the deceased held high ritual status. The set of seventeen Pukumani poles now at the Art Gallery of New South Wales was made at Milikapati in 1958.   69

Large painted bark baskets called *jimwalini* are often thrust through the tops of the poles at the graveside. Bama Yu's basket demonstrates an effective use of the *pwata*, a comb made from a flat piece of wood or bark with several teeth, used for making lines of dots. The Tiwi do not weave fibres, and carrying-baskets are made of folded and sewn sheets of bark which are then painted. Other ceremonial trappings of the Pukumani are elaborately carved and painted spears and a range of arm- and headbands including the *pamijini*, a wide circular band with feathered tassels. The exceptionally fine and old example shown here   71

70

87

is made from fibres, feathers and red abrus seeds. Similar arm- and headbands are still made today.

Since the 1930s the Tiwi have been renowned for painted figurative sculpture, a development from the Pukumani pole, and more recently for sculptures of animals and birds. Enraeld Djulabiyanna's double-sided figures of *Purukuparli and Bima* owe much to the Pukumani pole tradition. The arms hang down from the figures' bulbous heads, while the negative space surrounded by the frame of the pelvis, the legs and the round base is similar to 'windows' carved into the poles.

The sculptural installation at the Museums and Art Galleries of the Northern Territory in Darwin interprets the creation period in eight episodes, ending with the death of Purukuparli. All the major characters are present, most in their animal or bird forms. The detail showing Bima carrying the child Jinani is the work of one of the foremost sculptors of the period, Mani Luki (Harry Carpenter). The other main artist to work on this group of sculptures was Paddy

72 Mani Luki (Harry Carpenter), *Bima carrying Jinani, c.* 1970, detail from the installation *The Purukuparli and Bima story*

73 (*right*) Enraeld Djulabiyanna, *Purukuparli and Bima, c.* 1955

74 (*far right*) Paddy Henry Ripijingimpi, *Bird*, 1979

Henry Ripijingimpi, also known as Teeampi, whose later figure 74
shows Tokwampini on the head of Purukuparli. The tiered
configuration is commonly found in Pukumani poles.

While sculpture is the main art form, paintings on flat sheets of bark 75
became more common during the 1960s with increased outside
interest in Aboriginal art. The pictorial art of the Tiwi is largely
esoteric and non-figurative. A wide variety of geometric designs are
used, and while many patterns recur, there is a large degree of
invention so that their interpretations rest very much with the
individual artists. Figurative images appear but rarely dominate a
composition. Tiwi graphic art is bold and colourful. The ochres used
are more friable than those found in Arnhem Land, and are therefore
crushed rather than ground in the preparation of paint. Traditionally,

75 Nellie Wanterapila, *Coral*, 1974

76 Declan Apuatimi, *Clubs*, c. 1984

77 Bede Tungutalum, Tiwi
Designs, *Yam design*, 1982 (detail)

brushes are made of frayed bark or feathers, and now European
brushes are also used. The distinctive *pwata* comb as well as a short
cylindrical stick supply the dots.

Nellie Wanterapila's *Coral* of 1974 reflects one of the activities that   75
are the domain of women – food collecting, in this case the gathering
of shellfish found on the coral reefs at low tide. The spirits of unborn
babies are said to reside in the shallow waters and coral reefs about the
islands, and this concept provides the spiritual dimension of the work.

One of the most respected, innovative and versatile artists of the
modern period was Declan Apuatimi. A great ritual leader, Apuatimi
possessed a broad visual vocabulary which he applied to sheets of
bark, ceremonial spears, animal sculptures, bark baskets, Pukumani
poles and carved figures. In the last two years of his productive life he
also painted several canvases. Since his death in 1985 a number of Tiwi   76
artists have taken up canvas, including Apuatimi's daughter Maria
Josette Orsto (born 1962).

78 Thecla Puruntatameri, *Irramaru*, 1991

While the traditional forms of art persist in contemporary times, since 1968 Tiwi artists have been at the fore in innovation, using new techniques and materials as vehicles for their rich pictorial heritage. The repertoire of Tiwi art has been expanded to include screenprinted cloth, batik, ceramics, printmaking and painting on paper apart from canvas.

In the late 1960s Bede Tungutalum and Giovanni Tipungwuti (born 1953) produced woodblock prints of totemic images. This led to other forms of printing, and in 1969 the company Tiwi Designs was established at Nguiu to produce screenprinted fabrics. Their bold and colourful designs continue to be based on traditional imagery. 77 *Yam design* by Tungutalum, for example, is an image drawn from the Kulama ceremony. The commercial success of the textiles led to the introduction of batik in 1988. In 1972 Tiwi Pottery was established by Eddie Puruntatameri (born 1947) and John Boscoe Tipiloura (born 1952) to enable artists to work in ceramics.

There is a general desire to experiment with new media among younger Tiwi artists. In the late 1980s several artists, principally women, adopted synthetic paints and gouache to revive old designs as well as create new ones. *Irramaru* by Thecla Puruntatameri portrays 78 the wedge-tailed eagle who introduced fire to the Tiwi world. The work is animated by the unusually dominant and dramatic rendition of the bird. Such innovations in treatment and materials are not introduced at the expense of other forms of art. Rather, they are an extension of the strong creative energies of Tiwi artists.

CONVERGENCE: THE ART OF WADEYE AND KIMUL

In contrast to the isolation and unique qualities of the Tiwi and their art, the Aboriginal communities at Wadeye (Port Keats) and Kimul 3 illustrate a convergence of cultural influences. The commencement of European mining and farming in the surrounding area in the 1870s had a deleterious impact on traditional life and led to migrations of people into the region. The Murrinh-Patha and other groups have established cultural links with Arnhem Land, the Victoria River district to the south and the eastern Kimberley.

Among the major Dreamings of the Murrinh-Patha is that associated with a manifestation of the Kunapipi religious cult known as Punj. Mutjingga the Ogress, the First Mother, is the focus of the Dreaming. The theme of swallowing and re-emergence is also present here. Mutjingga was left to look after the children of the other beings while they went in search of wild honey. During their absence Mutjingga swallowed several of the children and ran off. The parents tracked her down to a river bed and eviscerated her, to find their children still alive in her belly.

Prior to the emergence of bark painting in the region the most common forms of portable pictorial art included engraved and painted sacred wooden boards and stones similar to those used in the desert. In the 1950s, bark painting was introduced through the agency of the mission at Wadeye as a means of producing collectible art at a time when bark paintings, particularly those made in Arnhem Land, were in demand. The early barks usually depict images similar to those found on the wooden boards and stones. The iconography is highly conventionalized and features many of the elements found in desert art, in particular the use of sets of concentric circles, usually denoting place, and meandering lines for the journeys of the ancestors. The typically formal composition is seen in Charles Mardigan's *Billabongs*, depicting circular waterholes in the artist's 79 country at Yenmenni. The two rectangular pointed shapes at the

79 Charles Mardigan, *Billabongs*, 1961

centre top and bottom of the painting indicate the boundaries of Mardigan's clan estate.

A distinguishing feature of bark painting in the region is the extended palette favoured by most artists. This goes beyond the four basic colours found elsewhere – white, black, red and yellow – to include greens, purples and pinks made by mixing various combinations of pigments. *Dirmu* is the Murrinh-Patha name for the visually stimulating patterns and designs that are found in nature and also appear in paintings and engravings made for ceremonial purposes. The term *dirmu* indicates these patterns are not haphazard or accidental, but the ordered creations of the supernatural beings of the Dreaming. The composition of these designs reflects social and ceremonial arrangements.

At Wadeye, sheets of bark are often cut to imitate the oval shape of the ceremonial boards that artists are accustomed to decorating.

94

80 Simon Ngumbe, *Rainbow Snake and children*, c. 1972

81 Robin Nilco, *Water python and boomerangs*, 1990

Simon Ngumbe's *Rainbow Snake and children* is an example. The   80
painting depicts Kunmangurr the creator-being as the ubiquitous
Rainbow Serpent. The coiled shape reflects the Serpent's presence in
waterholes containing the spirits of unborn children, seen in the form
of snakes that frame its head. The subject of the work recalls the theme
of swallowing and regurgitation.

Robin Nilco's shaped canvas *Water python and boomerangs* is styled   81
on the oval barks used in the region. Again, the images are
symmetrically arranged, and include naturalistic representations as
well as conventional symbols. The land is shown in planar view with
creeks as the straight lines joining circular waterholes. Sets of
concentric dotted circles also indicate waterholes. Symbols of flowing
water appear as meandering lines decorating the fighting boomerangs
and the central line of the painting. The meander is reiterated in the
shapes of the water-pythons which are the artist's primary totem.

82 Nym Bunduk, *Map of the Murrinh-Patha countryside*, 1959

82 The most prominent Murrinh-Patha artist was Nym Bunduk, whose *Map of the Murrinh-Patha countryside* reflects the abundant knowledge of a painter who was also a major ceremonial leader. The work is a comprehensive conceptual survey of Murrinh-Patha country. Using conventional symbols, Bunduk traces the journeys of the ancestors who created the country and its topographical features. The work was produced at the request of the anthropologist W.E.H. Stanner who sought to investigate the artist's conception of his environment. To convey a subject of such all-embracing magnitude, Bunduk used a much larger board than was usual. The painting's fluid lines are a departure from the highly formal compositions on bark, and it displays many elements which were to appear some twenty and thirty years later in paintings by eastern Kimberley artists.

79, 145

The iconography and painting styles found in the paintings of Bunduk and other artists from the Wadeye and Kimul region connect the art of the top end of the Northern Territory with that of the Kimberley and, in the south, to the traditions of the central desert areas.

96

CHAPTER THREE

The art of place and journey: the desert

Vast regions of the central and western parts of the Australian continent, including much of the Northern Territory, South Australia and Western Australia, are covered by geographical deserts, a word which implies harsh and barren landscapes. The Australian deserts appear empty and inhospitable to those who do not know them, but to the Aboriginal groups who inhabit these areas, the lands created by their ancestors and infused with their powers are places rich in spiritual meaning and physical sustenance.

The deserts are also the home of one of the most important movements in contemporary Australian art, for, while artists continue the traditional practice of painting on the ground, on their material possessions such as shields, wooden dishes and boomerangs, and on their bodies, they now use acrylic paint and canvases to carry the classical idioms of desert art to a wider audience than was previously possible.

83
93, 104
95–103

Geographically, the desert includes mountain ranges and spectacular rock-formations, grassy plains, stands of eucalypt and mulga trees, lakes, salt pans, sandhills, and stretches of stony country occasionally broken by seasonal watercourses and rivers and punctuated by rare permanent rockholes, springs, waterholes and soakages. The region is home to a number of Aboriginal groups who in the main share common cosmology and social systems, as well as common art traditions, and who form a major cultural bloc in Aboriginal Australia. Across this landscape spreads a web of ancestral paths travelled by the supernatural beings on their epic journeys of creation in the Jukurrpa or Dreaming, linking the topography firmly to the social order of the people.

The impact of European incursions and settlement on the peoples of the Australian desert was different from that on Arnhem Land. The first European explorers entered central Australia in 1860, and by 1885 much of the best grazing land around present-day Hermannsburg was occupied by pastoralists. Cattle and sheep polluted waterholes, and the new land-holders forced many groups of Aboriginal people away from their traditional lands. Other adverse consequences of European settlement, such as the spread of new diseases and the influx of refugees from the newly settled areas, had an impact on Aboriginal groups right across the desert, in some cases nearly a century before they sighted Europeans for the first time. Nevertheless, Aboriginal people were able to continue their relationships to their lands despite the wholesale takeovers by working on the pastoral stations, and by ensuring the continuity of rich oral traditions and ceremonies through which the land was celebrated and vivified.

The physical dislocation accelerated in the twentieth century as settlement spread. In 1941 Haasts Bluff, west of Alice Springs, was declared a reserve, and by 1955 Government settlements were established at Yuendumu and Lajamanu, with the last settlement of the assimilation era created at Papunya in 1960. Until 1966, under Government policies Aboriginal people were taken to live in these settlements, bringing them together in the most inappropriate social circumstances with detrimental effects on their cultural practices.

Federal political changes of the 1970s permitted and even encouraged people to return to live on their ancestral lands. Today, the desert towns of Papunya, Yuendumu, Lajamanu and others service many, often distant outstations that have sprung up since 1970. The Aboriginal councils in these towns have established cooperatives to cater for artists' needs, and to channel art from the outlying areas to the galleries of the cities. The cooperatives operate as buffers between the traditional social and cultural concerns of the artists and the demands and expectations of the outside world.

Classical desert art takes many forms, from decorated weapons and implements to personal adornments, from sacred and secret incised boards and stones, often called *tjurunga*, to rock engravings and paintings, and the more ephemeral arts of body painting, sand drawings, ceremonial constructions and ground paintings. While the classical traditions continue, the introduced media such as acrylic paint and canvas are usually employed for the purposes of public art.

Recently introduced techniques of dating rock engravings, and the persistence of similar painted images recorded in the nineteenth century, reveal that designs that are commonly in use today for both ceremonial and public paintings have been continuously produced in the desert for many millennia.

The basic elements of the pictorial art are limited in number but broad in meaning. The iconography of desert art is a language separate and distinct from that of Arnhem Land. Characteristic of the range of conventional designs and icons are those denoting place or site, and those indicating paths or movement. Concentric circles may 90, 112 denote a site, a camp, a waterhole or a fire. In ceremony, the concentric circle provides the means for the ancestral power which lies within the earth to surface and go back into the ground. Meandering and straight lines may indicate lightning or water courses, or they may describe the paths of ancestors and supernatural 102 beings. Tracks of animals and humans are also part of the lexicon of desert imagery. U-shapes usually represent settled people or breasts, while arcs may be boomerangs or wind-breaks, and short straight lines or bars are often spears and digging sticks. Fields of dots can indicate sparks, fire, burnt ground, smoke, clouds, rain, and other phenomena.

The interpretations of these designs are multiple and simultaneous, and depend upon the viewer's ritual knowledge of a site and the associated Dreaming. The meanings are elaborated and enhanced by the various combinations or juxtapositions of designs in the paintings, and also by the social and cultural contexts within which they operate – whether for ceremony or the public domain, for instance. The combinations of designs allow an endless depth of meaning, and artists in describing their work distinguish between those meanings which are intended for public revelation and those which are not, and provide the appropriate level of interpretation. Certain conventional compositional structures and pictorial devices are favoured by particular groups but, unlike the case in areas of Arnhem Land, may refer not just to one but to a number of different Dreamings. 111

Men's religious designs are called *kuruwarri* in Warlpiri, and 107–9 women's *yawulyu*. The terms refer to designs which represent the 87–8 ancestral beings, or any marks which indicate their presence. The 113 terms also embrace wider concepts to include the procreative essences or powers of the ancestors. The term *yawulyu* is also used for certain women's ceremonies, and although *yawulyu* images may refer to the same ancestors as the men's designs, they are usually concerned with notions of sexuality, fertility, well-being and growth among people, natural species and the land. *Kuruwarri* and *yawulyu* designs include 106, 114 many of the same graphic elements; their differentiation depends on the particular male or female contexts in which the designs operate.

Both kinds of designs possess tactile qualities; in many circumstances they are incised into wood or stone, drawn by hand into the sand or painted on to people's bodies. Texture and colour are integral components of desert art. Birds' down and fibrous substances obtained from plants are mixed with ochre and applied to people's bodies and objects, and used in ground paintings. Colours are significant in themselves, in the ritual associations of the site where they were obtained, and in their particular lustre or dullness. Artists seek similar qualities in the synthetic paints that are available today.

In the traditional social structures of the desert, the kinship system places each member of the society in one of up to eight categories which are paired for joint custodianship of the subjects of art – the land, ceremonies and Dreamings. For males, the paired kinship groups are termed Jampijinpa and Jangala, Jakamarra and Jupurrurla, Jungarrayi and Japaljarri, Japanangka and Japangardi. The prefix 'Na' (as in Nampijinpa) or 'Nu' supplies the term for the female equivalents. The pairings arise from patrilineal relationships, and people customarily include their kinship categories as part of their names.

To varying degrees across the desert, paired ceremonial roles are followed in the making of art for the public domain. Here as elsewhere in Aboriginal Australia, the collaboration between members of the opposite moieties is fundamental in the production of art for ceremony. In the desert those with patrilineally inherited rights in land, ceremonies, Dreamings and associated designs, i.e. the owners, are termed *kirda* (again in Warlpiri), while those with matrilineally inherited rights are known as *kurdungurlu*. An individual is *kirda* of certain ceremonies and *kurdungurlu* of others. In the making of public art, however, *kirda* may often act singly, or with the assistance of *kurdungurlu*. The practicalities of everyday life also allow for collaboration between those in other family relationships, such as husband and wife, parents and children, and siblings. On occasion, and with the appropriate permission from the owner of the Dreaming, people will make paintings alone of themes to which they are in a *kurdungurlu* relationship.

Among the most spectacular art forms of the desert are the large ceremonial ground paintings or mosaics made from earth-pigments and other natural materials on a prepared soil surface. Ground paintings are usually of a highly sacred and often secret nature, but some have been made in public contexts. In 1989 a group of six artists from Yuendumu installed a Yam Dreaming painting, *Yarla*, in the exhibition *Magiciens de la terre* organized by the Centre Georges Pompidou in Paris. As a concession to the context the artists confined the painting within a rectangular shape, as occurs on canvas. A feathered pole emerging from a set of concentric circles was the focal

83

83 Paddy Jupurrurla Nelson, Paddy Japaljarri Sims, Paddy Cookie Japaljarri Stewart, Neville Japangardi Poulson, Francis Jupurrurla Kelly and Frank Bronson Jakamarra Nelson, *Yarla*, ground painting installed in Le Halle de la Villette, Paris, May to August 1989

point of the work. Covering an area of forty square metres, the work provides an indication of the potential size of ground paintings.

Ground paintings provided one of the models for acrylic paintings on canvas and board which initially emerged around 1970. Yet, the first recorded example of innovation in desert art intended for sale appeared in 1903. *Toas*, small assembled sculptures made of carved wood, gypsum, ochres and other natural materials, were made by the local Diyari and other language-speakers at the Lutheran Mission at Killalpaninna, near Lake Eyre in South Australia. More than four hundred *toas* were made between 1903 and 1905 in response to the wish of the missionary, Pastor Johann Reuther, to build a collection of Aboriginal artefacts to raise funds for the mission. The *toa* collection was acquired by the South Australian Museum in 1907, but it appears that their production had ceased when Pastor Reuther left the mission in 1906.

The popular belief that Aboriginal culture was static encouraged the view that the *toas* were a traditional form of sculpture. The Diyari themselves described them as direction-markers or signposts that were left at abandoned camps to inform the next visitors of the

84 Various artists, *Group of toas*, 1904-5

ancestral nature of the landscape, or to indicate where the previous party had gone. However, it appears the *toas* were purely innovative works with no recorded antecedent in traditional life, although they embody a prevailing system of iconography and meaning. Of the *toas* illustrated, the third from the right depicts a deep waterhole (a dark vertical ovoid) on Cooper Creek. The arc above represents the waterhole, and the dotted knob a sandhill where the ancestor Patjalina hunted. By way of contrast, the seventh *toa* from the left shows, in a summary and naturalistic manner, a standing pelican, one of a flock seen by the ancestor Mandramankana, at a lake represented by the white band under the pelican's head.

    In many ways, the *toas* set a precedent for Aboriginal artists across the desert. Sculpted objects were the first forms of portable art to be made specifically for the public domain.

    The influx of non-Aboriginal people into the desert gathered momentum with the opening of the trans-Australia railway in 1915. Missions were established in the Warburton Ranges in 1934 and at Ernabella in 1939, and Aboriginal people were encouraged to produce wood carvings for sale to the mission shops in the cities. Uluru (Ayers Rock) opened up for tourist travel after World War II, and the boom in tourism since 1980 has provided a steady market for Aboriginal artefacts.

Much of the public art in the southern desert made since outside interest in Aboriginal art increased in the 1970s has been produced by women. The men have been generally more reluctant to produce public paintings, though both men and women make plain and decorated wooden carvings of animals, carrying-bowls, digging and music sticks and clubs. Artists have adapted introduced tools and materials to their needs; for instance, heated fencing-wire provides the means to burn or brand linear designs on to the carvings. The images belong to traditional idioms, but the new techniques allow for more innovative interpretations of *kuruwarri* and *yawulyu* designs.

Women traditionally spin animal-fur and human hair into cord with which to make skirts, belts, and headbands and head-rings for carrying-bowls. Since 1948, Pitjantjatjara women at Ernabella have spun and woven sheep's wool into products ranging from traditional carrying-bags to non-traditional belts, scarves and floor rugs. These items incorporated designs which the Pitjantjatjara women also produced in crayon drawings and watercolours based on *yawulyu*. The production of weavings was largely replaced by fabric dyeing after the introduction of batik techniques in 1972. The use of the *canting* (wax pen), paintbrushes, waxes and dyes allowed for new elaborations on *yawulyu* on silk and cotton fabrics. Angkuna Graham's fabric-length *Untitled* is characteristic of Pitjantjatjara batik designs; it shows organic forms based on leaves, flowers and plants, composed in a manner which owes something to the traditional Javanese batiks with which several Ernabella artists had become familiar. The arrangement also relates to the formal compositional structures of contemporary acrylic paintings. While many of the paintings, especially those by men, take an expansive and heroic view of country, the women's batiks build images based on a knowledge of the more intimate details of the land.

85 Unknown artist, *Animal carving*, 1977

86 Angkuna Graham,
Ernabella Arts, *Untitled*, 1984

OPPOSITE

87 (*above*) Kay Tunkun,
*Kipara (Wild Turkey)
Dreaming*, 1986–87

88 (*below*) Sadie Singer,
Summer landscape, 1988

The success and popularity of the work of the Ernabella women encouraged others in the neighbouring communities of Fregon, Indulkana, Amata, and even as far away as Utopia to take up batik and other introduced techniques.

3, 119

The experimentation and innovation in the use of colour and designs evident in the early Ernabella paintings continues today. From Fregon in South Australia, Kay Tunkun's watercolour *Kipara (Wild Turkey) Dreaming* combines florid forms and dotted circles suggesting ceremonial *yawulyu*. Sadie Singer was among the first group of artists to take up linocut prints at Indulkana in 1981. She has since developed other printmaking techniques through workshops outside the community. In the lithograph *Summer landscape* the *yawulyu* is similar to designs traditionally drawn in the sand to accompany narratives told by women.

87

88

In the 1930s, watercolour landscape painting in the European vein was introduced by Rex Batterbee, a non-Aboriginal artist, to Aboriginal people at the Lutheran Mission at Hermannsburg, west of Alice Springs. It was taken up by Albert Namatjira, who became Australia's first popularly known Aboriginal artist. In the era of assimilation, Namatjira's mastery of European techniques was interpreted as evidence for the potential success of this policy. The school of painting which developed among the Arrernte at Hermannsburg continues to produce watercolours today.

89

For all his success, Namatjira's achievements were dismissed as derivative by art commentators until the recent re-assessment of his work in the modern era of Aboriginal art. Namatjira is now seen to have reworked the models of European pictorial perspective to express his personal vision. His subjects were not chosen for their ostensible beauty in European terms, as had been thought, but were ancestral landscapes through which he expressed his personal relationship to the country to which he was spiritually bound. Namatjira's images are of the land created in the Dreaming, untamed by the requirements of the pastoral industry and by other evidence of European settlement.

Namatjira held his first solo exhibition in 1938, but despite his fame, he died disillusioned by white society. Nonetheless, Namatjira had made a major contribution towards changing negative public perceptions of Aboriginal people and laid the groundwork for the acceptance of more recent developments in Aboriginal art, particularly in the desert, where the Papunya school of painting emerged twelve years after his death.

89 Albert Namatjira, *Anthewerre*, c. 1955

THE PAPUNYA PAINTING MOVEMENT

Papunya is the birthplace of one of the most significant movements in   3
modern Australian art, for it was here that, in 1971, Aboriginal artists
transferred their ancestrally inherited designs and images into
synthetic paints on portable surfaces which were destined to leave the
local community. The wider appreciation of the richness of the art of
the desert commenced.

Papunya is situated at a site of the Honey Ant Ancestor. It was
established under the assimilation policy in 1960 for a number of
groups including Arrernte, Anmatyerre, Luritja and southern
Warlpiri, but principally Pintupi people, all of whom have ritual
connections with the Honey Ant Dreaming. The transition from a
semi-nomadic life of camps to a sedentary one had been very rapid
and harsh. As a result, Aboriginal people had neither the power to
determine their own futures, nor a voice with which to express their
aspirations to the outside world.

A catalyst for change was an art teacher, Geoffrey Bardon, who
arrived to teach children in the school in Papunya in 1971. After a

while, Bardon encouraged the school yardmen and other local elders to join in painting a mural in the traditional mode on the walls of the school. The issue of making a public painting using traditional images caused much debate among the older men. Such designs had previously only been painted on to rock walls, objects and participants' bodies in ceremony, and in related ground paintings. Eventually Old Tom Onion Tjapangati, the owner of the Honey Ant Dreaming, gave permission for Billy Stockman Tjapaltjarri, Long Jack Phillipus Tjakamarra, Kaapa Tjampitjinpa, Old Mick Tjakamarra and other artists to paint the mural. Other murals followed, although after Bardon left Papunya in 1972 they were destroyed under regulations intended to keep the school pristine.

Nonetheless, the successful completion of the murals encouraged other local artists to paint. Sympathetic to their aspirations, Bardon provided the new materials of synthetic paints and boards. Kaapa Tjampitjinpa (1920–89), who had occasionally made similar paintings on board prior to Bardon's arrival, was the main protagonist in the painting movement that followed. The Papunya Tula Artists' Cooperative was formed during Bardon's stay to look after the artists' interests.

The movement at Papunya has developed through a number of phases, marked by changes in style, technique and type of imagery. While the range of colour in ground paintings could go beyond ochres, pipeclay and charcoal to include other colours derived from natural materials, the synthetic paints offered a wider palette than that previously possible. The artists experimented with the newly available colours: orange, red and pink found favour for a while, but by and large the palette remained restricted until about 1980 when a wider range of colours again became common. Synthetic paints also reproduced the qualities associated with the use of natural pigments, such as the luminosity sought in ceremonial painting, and their quick-drying properties are indispensable for artists who usually work in the open air.

91, 92 The first paintings were small, and painted flat on the ground or on the artist's lap. The rectangular boards would be turned around and painted from all sides if necessary, like bark paintings in Arnhem Land. The planar nature of the works and the consequent lack of a horizon line in the European style of landscape painting, makes the viewing orientation of minor significance, unless otherwise implied by the artist. The relationship between the arrangement of elements in the paintings and the cardinal points of the compass conveys greater

90 Billy Stockman Tjapaltjarri, Long Jack Phillipus Tjakamarra, Kaapa Tjampitjinpa, Old Mick Tjakamarra and other artists, *Honey Ant Dreaming*, 1971, mural at Papunya School

meaning, as the latter are commonly used in the description of distant people and places, and the direction of the travels of the Dreaming beings.

Within the first three years of the movement, the size of the boards increased and artists moved to painting on canvases which could be rolled and transported with ease. As with the boards, the canvases are painted lying flat. 94 97

Originally painters employed a combination of naturalistic or schematic depictions of objects such as shields, spears, axes and sacred emblems used in men's secret ceremonies, with more conventional symbols, all usually painted against monochrome, often dark backgrounds. Human figures in full ceremonial regalia and body designs were also represented at one stage. However, the classical pictorial language of the desert seldom includes such naturalistic representations. In the traditional context, conventional iconography painted on to an object makes it unnecessary to depict the object itself. The fact that imagery of a sacred and secret nature could be broadcast to a public who did not possess rights to the deeper significance that it 91 encompassed was beyond the experience of the painters. This realization prompted artists to develop mechanisms to render their paintings appropriate for the public.

91   In *Children's Kadaitcha Dreaming*, Long Jack Phillipus Tjakamarra depicts the decorated figure of the Kadaitcha or law-enforcer at the top of the painting, and the decapitated body of a transgressor below right. The painting also includes conventional imagery, such as the three sets of concentric circles representing the Kadaitcha's fires and the wavy lines for smoke. The theme of the painting is didactic, and it is intended for the education of young children. Like outsiders, children are not initiated, and so the painting has been deemed suitable by the artist for public display.

By 1974 the naturalistic elements in paintings became less frequent and the narrative was expressed through conventional symbols which, given their multi-referential range of meanings, allowed the artists to describe their work without reference to secret information. Thus the public story could be separated from the more esoteric

92   meanings. Charlie Tjararu Tjungurrayi's *Mitukatjirri* dispenses with overtly naturalistic images. It describes the creation of a landscape by ancestors who performed ceremonies at the site which contains a sacred cave. At a nearby unusual rock-formation, the male ancestors broke the law by having sexual intercourse with women of the wrong kinship group. The concentric circles joined by lines indicate the sites and the ancestral paths between them, while the other images relate to the geological formations and to the ancestors. The story is a warning about proper sexual conduct; it is also about the cataclysmic events leading to the creation of the land.

A feature of *Mitukatjirri* is the use of dots. In ritual painting dots are used to outline design elements, and so they appeared in the acrylic

94   paintings, until gradually artists extended their use to cover the entire picture surface. The use of dots or repeated marks in this way may have a number of origins, none of which is mutually exclusive. They may be intended to evoke the use of birds' down or fibrous fluff, or to imitate the process of making ground paintings. They have been used to indicate differences in topography and vegetation. Areas of dots may mask sacred designs, and they may be used to produce visually stimulating effects intended to evoke the presence of supernatural power in the earth. The broad use of dots creates a field within which the action in a painting takes place.

93   In the painted shield by Dinny Nolan Tjampitjinpa the dots intimate feathery down and relate to the subject of the work:

91 Long Jack Phillipus Tjakamarra, *Children's Kadaitcha Dreaming*, 1972

92 Charlie Tjararu Tjungurrayi, *Mitukatjirri*, 1972

93 Dinny Nolan Tjampitjinpa, *Shield*, 1972

Lyurulyuru, a small bird with a red breast, at Ingiri waterhole near Mount Doreen. The entire design suggests the bird's body. The concentric circles are the entrails, the main dark vertical is the back, while the shorter, horizontal lines indicate the sides. At another level, the concentric circles represent a camp and the dotted lines a landscape.

One of the masters of visual effects created by the overlaying of patterns of dots is Johnny Warrangula Tjupurrula. In *Nintaka and the Mala (Wallaby) Men* he carries the use of dots to the point where the iconographic elements dissolve into the field of the painting. The work concerns the creation of country through a series of epic events. Two large Wallaby Ancestors eat Matingpulangu, a large Dingo Ancestor, who in turn is restored by Luurnpa, a Kingfisher Man. The ancestors are represented by their tracks at the top right of the painting. The perentie or large lizard, Nintaka, is shown both naturalistically and by his tracks in the lower right. Three sites (the concentric circles) are surrounded by U-shapes indicating ancestors in human form. One of the sites, Tjikari, is the artist's birthplace, therefore the painting reflects the religiously ordained connection between himself, the ancestors and the land.

Among the Pintupi, who by the early 1980s had begun to return to their ancestral lands around Kintore and Kiwirrkura in the west, artists began to develop archetypal images constructed purely of concentric circles representing sites with journey lines joining them. The circles are often surrounded by U-shapes indicating the participants in the events depicted, and the areas in between are filled with contour-like parallel lines of dots. The device allows artists to compose pictures about highly esoteric subjects such as the Tingari ancestors (pp. 153–4). Anatjari Tjampitjinpa's *Ceremonial ground at Kulkuta* depicts a Tingari initiation ceremony. The larger sets of circles represent the body-designs of the older men who are painting the bodies of the young initiates, shown as smaller circles. The background stipple represents the cleared ceremonial ground, while around the perimeter of the painting the dots indicate a body of water surrounding the camp.

Anatjari makes minimal use of iconography to imply a wealth of concepts far deeper than the interpretation given to the uninitiated, and the device is taken to extremes in the work of other Pintupi painters. Ronnie Tjampitjinpa's *Two Women Dreaming*, for example, concerns two ancestral women who travelled to Pitijinpirri where they built a shade, represented by the white lines in the painting,

94 Johnny Warrangula Tjupurrula, *Nintaka and the Mala (Wallaby) Men*, 1973

within which they placed their coolamon or carrying-dishes, seen as the innermost rectangles. The indentations in the earth made by the coolamon became life-sustaining water soakages. The propensity for austere compositions among the Pintupi is exemplified by Turkey Tolson Tjupurrula's *Straightening spears at Ilyingaungau*, based on a pre-battle ceremony, while in *Bandicoot Dreaming* Mick Namarari Tjapaltjarri practically dispenses with dots to show the scratch-marks made by Tjakalpa the desert bandicoot as it digs its burrow at the Dreaming-site of Putja.

96
98

Uta Uta Tjangala was an influential artist who lived in the area around Kintore. His *The Old Man's Dreaming* is another Tingari subject which concerns the punishment of a man who had a sexual affair with his mother-in-law. The painter has dispensed with many of the graphic symbolic elements. Joined circles represent sites visited in the saga, while the larger ovoids represent the rock formations at the site of Yumari. The powerful composition reflects the cataclysmic forces that created the landscape. Offsetting the summary elements is a

99

95 Ronnie Tjampitjinpa, *Two Women Dreaming*, 1990

96 Turkey Tolson Tjupurrula, *Straightening spears at Ilyingaungau*, 1990

meandering path that leads from a site to the figure of the Old Man, his body painted in designs.

By way of contrast to the austere compositions favoured by Pintupi painters, artists such as the Anmatyerre/Arrernte brothers Clifford Possum Tjapaltjarri and Tim Leura Tjapaltjarri create rich painted surfaces and employ a wide range of the available iconography. Clifford Possum's *Honey Ant Dreaming story* and Tim Leura's *Men's camps at Lyrrpurrung Ngturra* embody formal compositions to make connections between land and ceremony. 101, 100

The ultimate meanings of these two works, however, are diametrically opposed, and they serve to illustrate artists' capacity to combine religious and aesthetic concerns with another level of personal expression.

Clifford Possum's *Honey Ant Dreaming story* depicts camps at ceremonies connected with the Honey Ant Ancestor at Karrinyarra, a 101

97 Anatjari Tjampitjinpa, *Ceremonial ground at Kulkuta*, 1981

site to the north of Papunya. Lines of men's camps alternate with those of the women. Large ceremonies are usually held at a time of plenty after the rains, when the land is capable of supporting large numbers of people in one place. The richness of the land is indicated by the presence of the grubs which are depicted along opposite edges of the painting and around the camps. The two light-coloured horizontals, which form a compositional device in much of Clifford Possum's work, represent the morning mists that spring up at the site at this

116

98 Mick Namarari Tjapaltjarri, *Bandicoot Dreaming*, 1991

99 Uta Uta Tjangala, *The Old Man's Dreaming*, 1983

100 Tim Leura Tjapaltjarri, *Men's camps at Lyrrpurrung Ngturra*, 1979

101 Clifford Possum Tjapaltjarri, *Honey Ant Dreaming story*, 1983

time of year. The painting reflects seasonality, the cyclical nature of   101
good seasons, and concentrations of people and ceremony.

Similarly, Tim Leura's *Men's camps at Lyrrpurrung Ngturra* is   100
concerned with formal ceremonial arrangements. An ancestral
Hunter, represented at the centre of the painting by the large U-shape
and his weapons, is seated at the major ritual camp. Other ritual
participants are shown in the surrounding camps. A snake and a
goanna represent the Hunter's entire catch – the land which had once
been rich in resources such as kangaroo and emu was now
impoverished. Leura's work carries the sense of melancholy engen-
dered by the hostile and destructive intrusions of European culture
upon his country. Characteristic of Leura's work, *Men's camps* is
painted in washes of dark colours, heightening the sense of
oppression.

Napperby Death Spirit Dreaming, Leura's major painting, is seven   102
metres long and made with the assistance of his brother Clifford
Possum. It was commissioned by Bardon, and depicts the journey
through the artist's life and country. The painting features a path-line
meandering between circular resting places, and major Dreamings of

102 Tim Leura Tjapaltjarri with Clifford Possum Tjapaltjarri, *Napperby Death Spirit Dreaming*, 1980

the artist are shown in three vignettes. From left to right, these are the Old Man's Dreaming, the Yam Dreaming and the Sun and Moon Dreaming. The spears and a boomerang indicate the presence of the great ancestral Hunter. The spirit of death, a skeleton, is shown nearing the end of the journey.

Although it is common for artists to depict one Dreaming in a painting, exceptions such as Tim Leura's *Napperby Death Spirit Dreaming* have appeared since the early days of the Papunya movement. Michael Jagamarra Nelson's country near Vaughan Springs lies at the intersection of several major Dreaming paths, and consequently his paintings integrate a number of these. In *Five Dreamings* the central horizontal represents the Dreaming-path of the Flying Ant, Pamapardu; the circles at the bottom left and top right are Possums at Jangankurlangu and Mawurji, while the tracks at the lower right are those of the two Kangaroo Ancestors at Yintarramurru. The circles at the lower right represent Mirrawarri, a Rain Dreaming site near Mount Doreen. The snake is Warnayarra the Rainbow Serpent at Yilkirdi near Mount Singleton. Concentration of

103 Michael Jagamarra Nelson, *Five Dreamings*, 1984

104 Sonder Nampitjinpa,
Pankalangu ceremonies at Yamunturnga, 1987

several Dreamings in one painting reflects the seniority of the artist in
the religious life of the region, and so his individual status. Jagamarra
Nelson also intimates the connections he has with Aboriginal groups
beyond his country, with whom he shares these Dreamings.

   In *Five Dreamings* Jagamarra Nelson was assisted by his wife
Marjorie Napaljarri. At Papunya, women were rarely acknowledged
to have had a hand in the production of paintings until about 1979.
Among the first to be recognized in her own right was Sonder
104   Nampitjinpa. *Pankalangu ceremonies at Yamunturnga* is a painted
coolamon (carrying-dish) depicting ceremonial camps and women,
represented by the arcs, sitting in formal arrangements. Nampitjinpa
also paints on canvas; her painted dish of 1987 recalls a time in the early
1970s when boards for painting were sometimes in short supply, and
artists would paint on sculptures, objects, even linoleum tiles instead.
Pansy Napangati was taught to paint by her relative Johnny
Warrangula in the early days of the movement. She now lives in Alice
Springs, but retains her links with her inherited land through her
105   paintings. *Old Man at Ilpilli* also depicts a ritual scene: the central
roundel is the waterhole at Ilpilli, while the three U-shapes, rather
than representing three individuals, are a single elderly Tjakamarra
man with his spear, boomerangs and hair-belt, at different stages of
performing his own ceremony.

106   Similarly, *Flying Ant Dreaming at Wantungurru* by Maxie Tjampitjinpa relates to ceremonial events, as indicated by the regular
arrangement of the icons. The circles indicate the holes in the earth
from which the ancestral termites known as Flying Ants emerge to
perform their creative acts. The roundels with bars to each side are

designs painted on the bodies of the key participants in ceremonies. The termites swarm in nuptial flights after the rains, and are associated with fertility and reproduction. This richness is evoked by Tjampitjinpa's characteristic areas of stippled paint which are comparable to the washes of paint applied to people's bodies and objects in ceremony.

The Warlpiri artists discussed above, and especially Michael Jagamarra Nelson, Sonder Nampitjinpa, Dinny Nolan and Maxie Tjampitjinpa, have had a considerable impact on the Papunya movement. However, the traditional lands of the Warlpiri also include a vast area of the Northern Territory to the north of Papunya, incorporating the settlements of Nyirrpi, Yuelamu, Willowra, Yuendumu and Lajamanu. 103-4, 93
106

3

WARLPIRI ARTISTS OF YUENDUMU AND LAJAMANU

The origins of the painting movement at Yuendumu, and subsequently in other Warlpiri settlements, were markedly different from those at nearby Papunya. Watercolours and acrylic paints had been made available to artists here in the early 1970s, when the Papunya movement was still in its infancy, but the Warlpiri were reluctant to reproduce ancestral designs for a wider public. When the artists at Yuendumu did eventually decide to take up the new materials in the early 1980s, they benefited from the experiences of their neighbours.

Yuendumu artists were more aware of the art market process from the outset. It was understood that their works would be kept publicly and permanently, rather than be ephemeral statements. Lengthy debate amongst the elders ensured that mechanisms were in place to permit only the transmission of the secular and public aspects of their imagery. In 1985, the cooperative Warlukurlangu Artists Association was formed to act as a vehicle for the implementation of this policy, and to channel the work into the public domain. The fact that the artists belong predominantly to one language-group, the Warlpiri, has facilitated the adoption of traditional social procedures in the organization. As a consequence, the collaborative methods of producing traditional art forms (see p. 100) are more common in the production of acrylic paintings, and the co-artists are usually acknowledged.

Also in contrast to the events at Papunya, in 1983 the principal of the Yuendumu school, Terry Davis, actively encouraged a group of

105 Pansy Napangati, *Old Man at Ilpilli*, 1990

107   senior men to paint the doors of the school with major Jukurrpa or
      Dreamings of the area. The elders regarded this as an opportunity to
      remind the students of their religious heritage and identity, and to
      provide a context for the non-Aboriginal values they encountered at
      school.

The painting of the doors was seen as an affirmation of cultural
strength, and gave the artists the opportunity to work on a scale and
within a time-frame which corresponded with traditional ritual
practices. Each door was painted within a short period of time, just as
ritual requirements would dictate a certain speed of execution, and the
resultant images were bold and painterly. *Ngapakurlu (Rain)* by
Paddy Japaljarri Sims illustrates an encounter between two ancestral
Rain Beings who were strangers to each other. The first Rain Being
travelled north of Yuendumu, camping at Jurntiparnta, a waterhole
belonging to Sims' mother's father, and struck the ground with bolts
of lightning. From small clouds, the Rain Being created people who
are the ancestors of the current owners of this land. Tiring from its
exertions, the Rain Being transformed itself into clouds. In the north it

124

106 Maxie Tjampitjinpa, *Flying Ant Dreaming at Wantungurru*, 1988

107 Paddy Japaljarri Sims,
Ngapakurlu (Rain), 1983

108 (*right*) Darby Jampijinpa Ross,
Emu Dreaming, 1987

met a second Rain Being which it covered with its cloud-form, and sending down a deluge, it entered the ground as a stream. In the painted door, the dominant zig-zag represents lightning, the inverted U-shapes clouds and the dots rain. The Dreaming narrative is continued in the paintings on other doors.

107

The Yuendumu school door-paintings provided a catalyst for the men to make paintings for the outside world. In the physical scale of the doors the artists recognized the potential to paint meaningful sequences of the Dreamings, rather than the details that small canvases

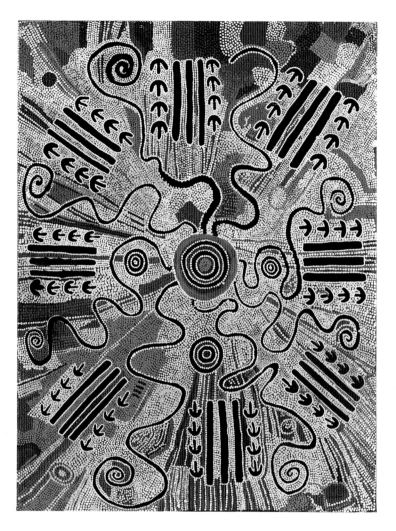

permitted. Three of the painters involved in the school project painted one of the first large canvases to leave Yuendumu. Jimmy Jungarrayi Spencer was the *kirda* or owner of the Dreaming depicted in *Yanjilypiri Jukurrpa (Star Dreaming)* of 1985. He supervised the painting but did not participate. Paddy Jupurrurla Nelson had matrilineally inherited rights to the Dreaming and was therefore the *kurdungurlu* and main painter, and he was assisted by Paddy Japaljarri Sims and Jimmy Jungarrayi Spencer's younger brother Larry Jungarrayi Spencer. The work concerns the Warlpiri fire ceremony

109

110 Liddy Napanangka Walker, Topsy Napanangka and Judy Nampijinpa Granites, *Wakirlpirri Jukurrpa*, 1985

associated with the creation of the constellations. The dynamic qualities of the painting became a hallmark of the earlier paintings by   109
men. *Emu Dreaming* by Darby Jampijinpa Ross is another such   108
example. Ross's work depicts several Emu ancestors, indicated by arrow-like footprints and the vigorous meandering lines which represent their intestines. The sets of bars represent spears and digging sticks, symbolic of men and women respectively, at the sites of Kunurrulypa and Ngunkurrlmanu.

Women artists have had a much more prominent role at Yuendumu than at Papunya, partly as a result of the interest shown in their work by the anthropologists Nancy Munn who first went to Yuendumu in 1956 and Françoise Dussart who worked there in the 1980s. Women had decorated mundane objects such as carrying dishes and digging sticks for sale prior to 1984, but in that year a group of elder women started to paint small canvases for sale in order to raise money for a vehicle which would allow them easy access to their often distant ceremonial grounds. The impulse to paint pictures thus arose from pressing cultural needs. In 1985, the year of *Yanjilypiri*   109
Jukurrpa (Star Dreaming), Liddy Napanangka Walker, Topsy Napa-   110

◀ 109 Paddy Jupurrurla Nelson, Paddy Japaljarri Sims and Larry Jungarrayi Spencer, *Yanjilypiri Jukurrpa (Star Dreaming)*, 1985 nangka and Judy Nampijinpa Granites collaborated to paint *Wakirl-pirri Jukurrpa*. The work depicts a Dogwood Dreaming site owned by Liddy, who painted the most prominent designs, and Topsy the *kirda* of the Dreaming. They were assisted by Judy who, although younger, is classed as their mother and is the *kurdungurlu*. The collaboration reflects the pattern of joint custodianship of the land which is expressed in art. Typical of *yawulyu* (women's designs), the painting celebrates the fertile aspects of the land. Women are depicted, as U-shapes, collecting the dogwood seeds and winnowing them. The seeds are half cooked, then washed in their *parraja* (carrying-dish) before being ground to a paste and made into damper (bread dough). The dominating images are three clusters of seed-pods. In contrast to the broad brushwork favoured by male artists at Yuendumu, women's paintings are characterized by dense, rich surfaces.

111   The Fire Dreaming at Warlukurlangu, depicted by Uni Nampijinpa Martin and Dolly Nampijinpa Daniels, was created by Lungkarda the Blue-Tongued Lizard Man to punish his two sons for killing a sacred kangaroo and not sharing the meat in the customary manner. The work concerns punishment of transgressors and the need to care for the land – in this case by firing the country as is the practice in many parts of Aboriginal Australia. This great fire was followed by torrents of rain which fertilized the land and caused all species of flora and fauna to thrive. The painting is composed to reflect formal ritual arrangements; between the two large curves representing windbreaks at either end of the canvas, the tracks of participants weave around circular ritual icons.

112   The ordered nature of creation is echoed in the structure of ceremonies and the composition of paintings. *Janganpa Jukurrpa (Possum Dreaming)* by Peggy Napurrurla Poulson, Maggie Napurrurla Poulson and Bessie Nakamarra Sims concerns the Possum Ancestor who created the waterholes of Warrkaparli, Lawanjajarra and Mawurji, represented by the three sets of concentric circles running vertically through the middle of the painting. All the action in the painting is focused on the circles. The straight and sinuous lines indicate the nightly journeys of the Possums from the main sites to others shown as circles between two U-shapes, and map the movements of performers in the ritual. The E-shaped icons represent the tracks of the Possum, and mark each of the journey-lines.

The dense tapestry of *yawulyu* in Jeannie Nungarrayi Egan's *Jardiwampa Jukurrpa (Snake Dreaming)* recalls sand drawings where designs depicting one episode of a story are wiped smooth and others

111 Uni Nampijinpa Martin and Dolly Nampijinpa Daniels (formerly Granites), *Warlukurlangu (Fire Country) Dreaming*, 1988

112 Peggy Napurrurla Poulson, Maggie Napurrurla Poulson and Bessie Nakamarra Sims, *Janganpa Jukurrpa (Possum Dreaming)*, 1988

are interposed. The work is a complex composition incorporating six 113 Dreamings located in an area between Ngarna to the south of Yuendumu and Katurnu to the north. The main image is the journey of the Snake Ancestors in human form, represented by the footprints along the upper edge of the painting. As they travelled, they danced and performed various rituals at camps along the way. The combination of Dreamings within the painting expresses the connections between kinship groups. For example, the Snake Dreaming belongs to the Nungarrayi-Napaljarri kinship group, while Kinki the Giant Woman Dreaming, represented by the large

113 Jeannie Nungarrayi Egan, *Jardiwampa Jukurrpa (Snake Dreaming)*, 1989

footprints at the upper left section of the painting, belongs to the Nakamarra-Napurrurla group.

One of the major Warlpiri Dreamings, Pamapardu or Flying Ant at Wantungurru, west of Yuendumu, belongs to the Nampijinpa-Nangala group. Flying ants or termites provide food and nesting areas for goannas and are also eaten by people, so signifying the fecundity of the land. The graphic quality of *Pamapardu Jukurrpa (Flying Ant Dreaming)* by Clarise Nampijinpa Poulson indicates her concern with the spatial organization of the Flying Ant ceremony, enclosed by two large arcs. The central set of concentric circles is at the same time the site at Wantungurru and the central construction on the ceremonial ground. The other sets of circles simultaneously represent smaller ceremonial camps and the termites' mounds, surrounded by the U-shapes of women who will collect the ants and their eggs.

Nampijinpa Poulson's treatment of the subject contrasts sharply with the atmospheric effect achieved by a male Warlpiri artist Maxie Tjampitjinpa in *Flying Ant Dreaming at Wantungurru*. Both works evoke the material and spiritual richness of the land within the artists' respective male and female spheres of ritual knowledge.

114

106

114 Clarise Nampijinpa Poulson, *Pamapardu Jukurrpa (Flying Ant Dreaming)*, 1990

3   Lajamanu, about four hundred kilometres north of Yuendumu, is a settlement established by the Government in 1947 to make way for mining and pastoral leases in the area. Although it lies well beyond traditional Warlpiri lands, in the following years Lajamanu was mainly populated by Warlpiri speakers from Yuendumu, many of whom were selected at random and taken there under Government regulations. The succeeding years saw a number of migrations between the two communities. Although many Warlpiri settled at Lajamanu and have established ritual links to the land they now occupy, contact with Yuendumu is constant. The Warlpiri at Lajamanu demonstrate the contemporary relevance of art by the fact that through painting they are largely able to fulfil their responsibilities to their ancestral lands which lie to the south and west and are difficult of access.

The genesis of the art movement at Lajamanu was slow. Here, too, artists were apprehensive about making art intended for the public domain, and they were concerned not to lose rights to their land through the exposure of religious secrets. Nonetheless, in 1983 twelve artists went to Paris to construct a ground painting and perform open ceremonies as part of the exhibition of contemporary Australian art entitled *D'un autre continent: L'australie, le rêve et le réel* at the Musée d'art moderne. In late 1985 a meeting of senior men gave approval for public paintings to be made. It was the men who created the first of these works, using house paint on large sheets of composition board, plywood and cardboard. At the same time women artists also began to paint, mainly in gouache on cardboard.

115   In 1986 a group of women produced a set of paintings for the local school at Lajamanu with much the same intention as the men at Yuendumu three years before. One of these was *Marsupial Mouse Dreaming at Marlungurru* by Molly Napurrurla Tasman which shows women of the Napurrurla and Nakamarra kin groups sitting down at Marlungurru. The large circles are the burrows of the Marsupial Mouse, the smaller circles depict the animal sitting and the Mouse's tracks are represented by the V-shapes. The work represents another variation in desert painting: the designs are concentrated so as to form the ground and contours of the picture surface. There is no space between the icons, no background.

Although they share the art traditions of Warlpiri elsewhere, the artists at Lajamanu favour freer compositions, emphasizing the strong graphic quality of the basic elements of desert iconography. Figurative elements and even animal and human footprints appear less

134

115 Molly Napurrurla
Tasman, *Marsupial Mouse
Dreaming at Marlungurru,*
1986

frequently than elsewhere in the desert. Images are usually set against a   117
background of uniformly coloured dots. The colours are austere,
with little of the subtlety achieved through the overlay of dotted
patterns. The compositions of the paintings are usually bold and
brash, while the pictorial detail common to many of the later
paintings at Papunya and Yuendumu is deliberately avoided.

Abie Jangala and Peter Blacksmith Japanangka were two of those   116–17
deeply involved with the Lajamanu painting movement from the
beginning. Jangala is one of the founders of the community.
Blacksmith was a senior ritual man with direct responsibility for the
country around Lajamanu.

Among the major Dreamings painted by men are water, rain,
clouds and thunder, and Jangala has ritual custodianship of many of
these Dreamings. His paintings are characterized by white back
grounds and a restricted palette, as can be seen in *Water Dreaming*. This   117
painting depicts an ancestral flood which originated at Mikanji near
Yuendumu, travelled to Puyurru and then branched out to Kulpu-
lunu and Kamira in the north. The waters washed through the

116 Peter Blacksmith
Japanangka,
Snake Dreaming, 1986

country and continued northwards until they reached the sea, linking the innermost regions of the Tanami desert with the coast.

116   The theme of water, the very source of life, is also the subject of Peter Blacksmith's bold and graphic *Snake Dreaming*. This depicts a Snake Ancestor and his brother who came from the west looking for water. They reached a place called Mundululu in Kurindji country where they encountered a number of Fish Ancestors who were suspicious of the Snakes and repelled them. The Snakes made for Wadjipilli, a waterhole near Lajamanu, in the artist's country. A rainbow, and then rain, followed the Snakes wherever they went, fertilizing the land.

118   The abundance of the land is celebrated in Jimmy Jampijinpa Robertson's *Seed Dreaming* which depicts two women, the large U-shapes in the painting, grinding seeds on rocks to make bread dough, while their children, shown as the smaller U-shapes, play a game of

117 Abie Jangala, *Water Dreaming*, 1987

118 Jimmy Jampijinpa Robertson, *Seed Dreaming*, 1986

snatching the seeds. The arabesques surrounding the scene represent   118
drying seed-pods and lend the work a dynamic quality in marked
contrast to the contemplative treatment of a similar subject in
Wakirlpirri Jukurrpa.   110

FROM SILK BATIK TO CAR DOORS: UTOPIA

The Anmatyerre and Alyawarre artists in and around Utopia in the   3
eastern part of central Australia have artistic traditions similar to those
of their western desert neighbours, despite differences in language and
social structure. Their land was taken over by pastoral leases or
stations in the 1920s, but some fifty years later the Anmatyerre and
Alyawarre began to re-occupy their traditional lands north and
north-east of Alice Springs. In 1979 they won back that part which
had been temporarily the Utopia cattle station. Instead of establishing
a central town or settlement, the Anmatyerre and Alyawarre prefer to
live in small outstations or camps, close to their ancestral country and
the spiritual sustenance it affords.

The rise to prominence of Utopia artists began with the making of
batik in the 1970s and continued with painting and other art forms as
these were introduced in the late 1980s. Through a series of specialized
education programmes commencing at the time of the move back to
their country in 1977, the women of the community were introduced
first to woodblock printing and tie-dyeing of fabric, and later in the
same year to batik.

The opportunity to gain a degree of economic independence
through the sale of batik, as well as the social nature of its production
which accords with local customs, led to the formation of the Utopia
Women's Batik Group in 1978. The Utopia women artists quickly
developed a preference for free drawing, using a brush for broad
areas, and the *canting* (wax pen) for fine work. As in Ernabella and
Fregon, the artists prefer to use silk fabric which enhances the fluidity   119–20
of the drawing. The designs of the batiks are mostly based on
ceremonial *awelye* (Anmatyerre for *yawulyu*, or women's designs)
which are applied to the breasts, arms and legs, and they often
incorporate naturalistic images based on the organic contours of
plants. Such designs are used as the vehicle to depict women preparing
for ceremony in Edie Kemarre's batik of 1987.   119

The history of the recent art of Utopia is punctuated by a series of
survey exhibitions. The first of these in 1988 was a collection of 88
batiks, including Sandra Holmes Kemarre's *Morning Star Dreaming*.   120

139

120   The work deals with an ancestral creation story concerning two Sky Brothers, the younger of whom had a stick with which they made a fire to cook a kangaroo. The brothers argued and the younger one fell into the fire and exploded, thereby creating the stars. The elder brother became the Morning Star. The batik image depicts the creation of the firmament which is mirrored in the landscape. Circles represent stones on the ground while the central circle is a waterhole.

The medium of painting was taken up in 1989 by artists in the second major survey exhibition, *A Summer Project*. As with later projects of woodblock prints and watercolours, the survey introduced a wide range of artists at Utopia to new media. Along with batik, painting has become the most popular form of art. The freedom of expression that the artists find in batik carries through into

119 Edie Kemarre, Utopia Women's Batik Group, *Women sitting in groups painting each other for corroboree*, 1987

paintings that range from highly formal compositions and narratives to works which dispense with conventional iconography of the desert altogether to incorporate naturalistic imagery and landscapes in the European manner.   124

Lindsay Bird Mpetyane, one of the few male artists to participate in the batik projects, was among the instigators of the move to painting in acrylic on canvas. His *Utnea* identifies the Snake Ancestor of that name with a site at Arremela, near the artist's home at Mulga Bore. The Snake is depicted both stretched out asleep and in motion. The short dashes represent the Snake's bones, which remain at this site and are tangible evidence of the ancestral events that occurred there.   122

An important leader of women's ceremonies, Emily Kame Kngwarreye, has emerged as one of the senior artists from Utopia.   123

120 Sandra Holmes Kemarre, Utopia Women's Batik Group, *Morning Star Dreaming*, 1988

Kngwarreye participated in the original Utopia Women's Batik Group and took up painting on canvas in her seventies. Her work is testimony to a lifetime of creating images. The designs in her batiks are usually composed of linear organic forms which cover the entire surface of the silk. In her paintings Kngwarreye uses these linear designs as a ground on which to lay fields of pure colour and dots. The paintings are based on *awelye* of plants, seeds and body painting. In

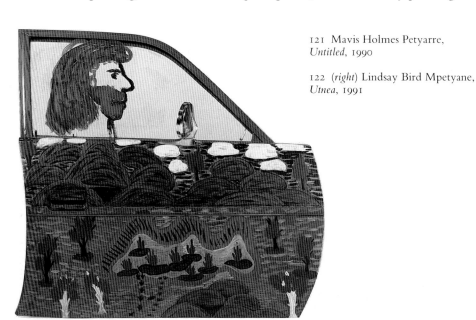

121 Mavis Holmes Petyarre, *Untitled*, 1990

122 (*right*) Lindsay Bird Mpetyane, *Utnea*, 1991

Untitled Kngwarreye creates a visual texture which evokes the physical and spiritual fertility of the land and the radiance of being that is sought in ceremony.

By way of contrast to Kngwarreye's minimal imagery, renditions of the landscape in the western perspectival manner are common in Utopia, in particular among artists working at the Antarrengenye outstation. *Sandover River* by Lilly Sandover Kngwarreye depicts the river of the artist's Dreaming. The formal composition of the river, the trees on the banks, the hills and the rising sun is offset by the repeated motif of parakeelya flowers across the canvas, indicating the artist's concern with the seasonal nature of the land rather than its topographical features alone.

Women's ceremonies are the subject of *Sacred grasses* by Ada Bird Petyarre. The plant-forms around the perimeter of the canvas point inwards to the centre of the work where a circle represents a ground painting. On either side of this circle are rectangular shapes described in dots which resemble a ceremonial ground. The painting indicates a planar perspective landscape, as though one were looking down on it from above, while at the same time the composition suggests the viewer is looking up through the ground as, indeed, the supernatural beings are said to view the world from their subterranean home.

Sculpture has become another popular form among Utopia artists. Sculpted objects such as men's shields and boomerangs and women's carrying dishes, digging and dancing sticks are part of the traditional creative output of the people of Utopia.

124 Lilly Sandover Kngwarreye, *Sandover River*, 1989

125 Ada Bird Petyarre, *Sacred grasses*, 1989

◄ 123 Emily Kame Kngwarreye, *Untitled*, 1991

Artists have also in the past carved wooden animal figures and decorated them with pokerwork designs. Figurative sculpture blossomed in 1989, and artists use the figures as a ground on which to apply painted designs. This concept is the basis for the Antarrengenye artist Mavis Holmes Petyarre's landscape painted on to a found object, an old car door. This work is yet another example of the degree to which Aboriginal artists are prepared to extend the parameters of the artistic traditions through experimentation and innovation.

121

CARING FOR DISTANT LANDS: BALGO

3 Balgo, on the edge of the Tanami and Great Sandy Deserts of Western Australia, was established in 1939 as a Catholic mission to cushion the effects of the developing pastoral and mining industries on the Aboriginal peoples of the region. The mission did not have such traumatic consequences for the local people as similar settlements elsewhere in the desert. The respect accorded Aboriginal customs and beliefs by the missionaries ensured their continuity.

The majority of those who moved to Balgo are Kukatja, Walmajarri, Warlpiri and Jaru language speakers. In cultural terms, the people of Balgo and the more recently established nearby settlements of Billiluna and Mulan are connected to the Pintupi and Warlpiri on the south and east, and to the Wangkajunga and Walmajarri whose land lies to the west in the Great Sandy Desert. They also have strong affiliations with the various groups in the Kimberley to the north. Not surprisingly, Balgo is a centre for major religious events.

The classical traditions of the art of Balgo are similar to those found elsewhere in central Australia. In the late 1950s soapstone and sandstone carvings of animals and objects were made, but this practice, briefly revived in 1981 and 1982, has since been discontinued, and painting is now the main art form.

Although from 1979 on a number of artists produced small portable paintings in acrylic and watercolour, the movement towards painting for an outside audience did not begin in earnest until 1986, with the exhibition *Art from the Great Sandy Desert* at the major art museum of Western Australia in distant Perth. Drawing on experiences of artists in other desert communities, those at Balgo keenly appreciated this opportunity to establish the nature of their relationship to the land in the eyes of the world at large. Significantly, one of the major contributors to the exhibition, Peter Sunfly

146

126 Peter Sunfly (Sandfly) Tjampitjin, *Sleeping at Naligudjana*, 1986

(Sandfly) Tjampitjin, was a senior Kukatja ritual leader. Tjampitjin emphasizes his authority over this country with works such as *Sleeping at Naligudjana*, which concerns two ancestral hunters (the   126 double U-shapes) camping in the sandhills of Balgo. The more recent paintings from Balgo continue to be modest in scale, and now most artists favour a palette of deep hues, often offset by raw colours to create densely animated surfaces.

Wimminji Tjapangarti was another for whom the significance of painting lies in its assertion of inherited authority over the country in the face of European intrusion. *The artist's country* shows the main   129 features of the land at Yapparry to the west of Balgo. The rectangles in the painting represent hills and claypans, with meandering creeks weaving their way around waterholes and soakages. One of the Tingari group of ancestors was an Old Woman who turned into a

127 Donkeyman Lee Tjupurrula, *Untitled*, 1989

small bird, and her tracks are depicted in the painting to establish the artist's connection with these ancestral beings.

127   The linear arrangement of the elements in Wimminji's painting is also evident in Donkeyman Lee Tjupurrula's *Untitled*. This work is a comprehensive map of his particular country, Walla Walla in the Pintupi lands close to Kiwirrkura. The painting focuses on the life-sustaining properties of water and important ceremonial sites. The major topographical features and the watercourses connecting them were created by the Tingari. Three large sets of circles represent major soakages which are also important ritual centres. They are surrounded by a string of lesser waterholes, joined by lines indicating rainfall and the grasses that provide the food-seeds which sprout after the rain. The significance of the sites depicted along the top of the painting is suggested by combinations of symbols: the sets of circles bracketed by black lines represent ceremonial places, while to the right an aggregation of symbols depicts caves in which the ancestral beings performed ceremonies, and where sacred objects are housed.

Experimentation and innovation in painting are more evident in

128 Susie Bootja Bootja Napangarti, *Kutal soakage*, 1989

128   the work of the Balgo women artists. Susie Bootja Bootja Napangarti creates a distinctive dynamism by emphasizing the diagonal journey lines which connect site-symbols in her paintings. In *Kutal soakage* the waterhole which is the home of a Rainbow Snake responsible for storms and lightning is depicted at the centre. The area is known for a particular marbled stone whose patterns make up the ground of the painting. The animated surface evokes the violent and turbulent nature of the being who resides there.

130   *The death of the Tjampitjin fighting man at Tjunta*, by the Warlpiri artist Patricia Lee Napangarti, relates the heroic events which led to ancestral energies entering the land at a site in her grandparents' country. A man of the Tjampitjin kinship group is shown as the inverted U-shape at the centre of the painting. A fearsome fighter, he stopped at a rockhole, the large circle at the top of the painting. The footprints in the smaller circle indicate the man standing in the water, drinking. He is challenged to a fight by a group of men shown by several U-shapes at the bottom. After a heroic battle the Tjampitjin succumbs to the wounds he receives. He is buried; the grave is shown as the oval shape on the right of the painting. Beneath the grave is a dish containing his hair which has been removed to be taken to his

129 Wimminji Tjapangarti, *The artist's country*, 1989

130 Patricia Lee Napangarti, *The death of the Tjampitjin fighting man at Tjunta*, 1989

mother and sisters who will spin it into a hair-belt, as is customary. The significance of the event, the land permeated by ancestral essence, is suggested in the juxtaposition of the icons against a highly innovative and energetic ground of dripped and splattered paint. Such inventiveness sits comfortably within the classical traditions of desert painting.

The richness, subtlety and vigour of the art of the desert has become widely appreciated since artists at Papunya found the means to render its distinctive visual language in portable, permanent materials, and artists in the other desert communities adopted similar methods over the following decade. While artists across the desert share a common artistic heritage, their work displays a variety of approaches in carrying the classical idioms beyond the region to the world at large.

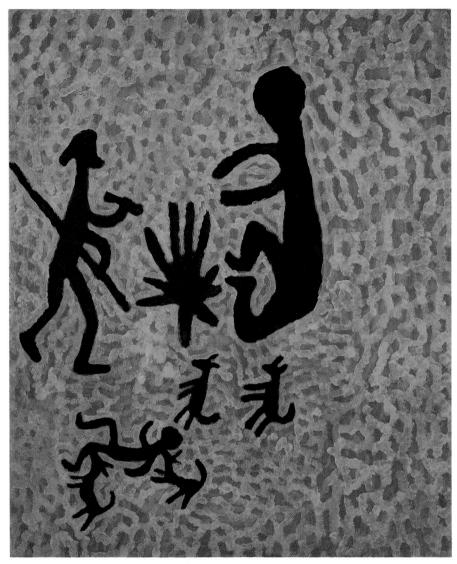

131 Jimmy Pike, *Jamirtilangu Parrija Purrku II*, 1987

CHAPTER FOUR

Land of the Wandjina: the Kimberley

The Kimberley region in the north-western corner of the continent is famous for the distinctive images of the Wandjina ancestors, but is also home to a variety of styles of art whose spread was determined by the patterns of traditional exchange-systems within the region. The diffusion process was accelerated from the end of the nineteenth century by the impact of European settlement and the changes this brought in the social conditions and mobility of the Aboriginal people.

3

135–7

The Halls Creek gold rush of 1886 and the establishment of the pastoral industry which followed led to the dislocation of Aboriginal family life and a series of massacres of Aboriginal people in the region. Despite this, traditional practices persisted as many Aboriginal people continued to live on their own lands, though now at the behest of the new pastoralist overlords. Forced migrations of people again became a reality in 1969 when laws granting equal wages to Aboriginal workers on the cattle stations resulted in wholesale evictions. People moved off the land to take up residence in towns and refuges.

The Great Sandy Desert is the ancestral home of the Walmajarri and related peoples. Their art is part of the continuum of the traditions of the desert, but also shows influences from the Kimberley and the central desert region. Many Walmajarri now find themselves living on land in the southern and eastern Kimberley to which they may have no ancestrally ordained connection, so that, as in Lajamanu and elsewhere in the desert, affiliations are formed to the local area and the connections with traditional lands are maintained largely through ceremony and its associated art forms.

134

THE TINGARI COME TO THE SOUTHERN KIMBERLEY

One result of the migrations was that religious cults associated with the great ancestral Tingari beings have spread from the western deserts to the region. Often regarded as a group of ancestral people with one or more dominant men or women, the Tingari travel across

132 Rhonda Lightning, *The Dingo and the Emu*, 1983

the land, and through events which occur at a particular location, provide the place with spiritual connotations.

In *The Dingo and the Emu*, Rhonda Lightning, a Jaru/Walmajarri artist from Halls Creek, has chosen an episode from the great journeys of the Tingari as a means of asserting his connection to his country near Balgo, more than two hundred kilometres to the south. As opposed to the generally non-figurative renditions of Tingari subjects among Pintupi painters, the naturalistic depiction of this subject together with the annotations indicates the explanatory nature of the work. It is intended to be read by outsiders. The transformative powers of the Tingari are expressed through the multiple images of the two Dingo Ancestors in both animal and human form. They chase the Emu Ancestor along Sturt Creek until they reach Lake Gregory near Mulan. In the painting the landscape is shown both in plan view and in profile, as though seen from the riverbed which runs laterally across the painting and branches out to Lake Gregory in the lower section.

The subject of *Moses and Aaron leading the Jewish people across the Red Sea* by Jarinyanu David Downs also relates to the Tingari. In much of Aboriginal Australia, people have integrated aspects of Christian mythology and the history of Europeans with models existing within their own cosmologies. Religious beliefs concerning the Tingari and associated beings provide ready models for Bible stories because of the Tingari's importance and the concepts of metamorphosis they incorporate. In Downs's painting, Moses and Aaron are distinguished by the size of their footprints, corresponding to the great powers they possess compared to ordinary people. Against this, the Egyptians and their horses are shown schematically, drowning in the arc of the sea. The chalice-like forms which frame the upper half of the painting represent burning bushes. Downs's work follows the pictorial conventions of desert painting in depicting travel across the land in relation to events at specific sites, and in the planar view of the land.

In the pastoral town of Fitzroy Crossing where Christianity has been a force in people's lives, Downs is both a religious leader of the

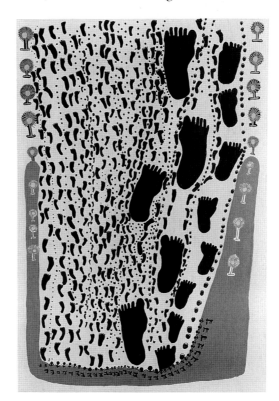

133 Jarinyanu David Downs, *Moses and Aaron leading the Jewish people across the Red Sea*, 1989

134 Peter Skipper, *Kurrkuminti Kurrkuminti*, 1987

Wangkajunga and Walmajarri groups and a Christian. Downs's artistic repertoire includes Dreaming themes of major ancestral beings, but a body of his work reflects a personal response to Christianity. For Downs, both religions serve similar purposes in revealing divine order in the cosmos.

The approach which draws on elements of the regional pictorial tradition and extends the parameters in a highly personal vision is characteristic of several artists of the region. It is especially evident in the work of Jimmy Pike, a Walmajarri man who comes from Japingka and spends much of his time in the Great Sandy Desert. Pike started to make art for the market in 1980, and his artistic activity includes a successful venture into the commercial world as a designer of fabrics for clothing and furnishings. His early work consisted of black-and-white linocuts and highly keyed non-figurative paintings whose designs are comparable to those found on engraved pearlshells that originate around Broome in the western Kimberley (p. 161).

131

Pike's more recent paintings and prints recount traditional religious themes of the creation of the country.

Jamirtilangu Parrija Purrku II illustrates part of an ancestral narrative in which social mores are linked to the creation of features of the landscape. The schematic images in the painting are set against a ground with no horizon, and depict a sequence of events. The painting concerns a boy who felt that he was constantly mistreated by his grandfather, recognizable as the face in profile with a beard and traditional hairstyle. The pair made a camp to shelter from an impending storm. The old man kept the best food for himself and took the driest spot, as befitted an elder. The boy refused to accept this arrangement, and an argument ensued. The boy ran away while the old man slept, taking his dogs and a firestick. In the morning the old man followed the boy and found him making camp, but the dogs attacked the old man and killed him. A rock in the sandhills marks the site of the attack, and is the transformed body of the old man.

THE WANDJINA

The central and northern areas of the Kimberley region are renowned for rock art which features the so-called Bradshaw figures, named for the European who first recorded them, and the more recent Wandjina images. Bradshaw figures bear some resemblance to the 'dynamic' or 'mimi' figures found on the rock walls in West Arnhem Land; they are usually small, monochrome, animated human images. It is difficult to judge the antiquity of these paintings, but they are believed to be at least three thousand years old, and they predate the larger polychrome images of the great Wandjina and associated beings. While the Bradshaw figures seem of little significance to recent generations of Kimberley people, the Wandjina are a constant source of inspiration in contemporary times. The recent migrations of Wororra and Ngarinyin people from the central and northern parts of the Kimberley, southwards and westwards to Derby and Mowanjum, have spread the influence of the Wandjina beyond their original boundaries.

'Wandjina' is a generic term for a group of ancestral beings who come out of the sky and the sea. They bring with them the rains, control the elements, and maintain the fertility of the land and natural species. They have shaped the features of the landscape, and left their images in ochres and white clay on the cave and rock walls of the region. These impressive images can be up to 6 metres (19 ft) long.

135 Wandjina figures painted on rock at Mandanggari on the Gibb River, Kimberley, Western Australia

136 Charlie Numbulmoore, *Wandjina-kaluru beings at Mamadai*, 1970

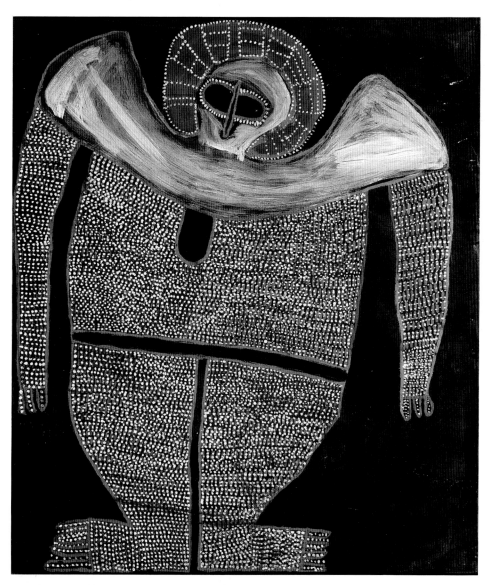

137 Alex Mingelmanganu, *Wandjina*, 1980

Artists belonging to the groups descended from the Wandjina regularly care for the images by repainting them to restore their brightness and preserve the spiritual essence of the ancestors, which is invoked in ceremony and in art.

A number of individually named Wandjina are distinguished, each with its own character and attributes. They exist along with a variety of associated beings such as benevolent and malevolent spirits, Lightning Men, women, pythons and other animal forms. Kaluru Wandjina are responsible for depositing the spirits of those to be born in waterholes.

136   *Wandjina-kaluru beings at Mamadai* by the Ngarinyin artist Charlie Numbulmoore shows the characteristic features of the Wandjina: the faces and bodies are white, the round black eyes have radiating lashes and, although the nose is indicated, the images are mouthless. The head is usually surrounded by a halo, thought to represent both the hair of the Wandjina and clouds, often with radiating lines which have been interpreted as feathers or the lightning controlled by the Wandjina. An oval shape in the middle of the chest may indicate the breastbone, although its form has affinities with pearlshell ornaments which originate in the western Kimberley. Not all Wandjina, however, have such a human form.

Images of Wandjina appear in a number of materials. They are painted on to slabs of sandstone and pieces of bark, engraved into pieces of slate coated with resin and cut into the hard shells of the nuts of the boab tree. Bark paintings seem to have first emerged in the Kimberley in the early 1930s in response to the demands of anthropologists working in the region. Paintings on bark were not produced on a regular basis until 1975, when stimulated by the work of Alex Mingelmanganu from Kalumburu, other artists in the region began to create characters or scenes drawn from their cosmological repertoire.

137   The imminent power of the Wandjina is expressed in the canvas by Mingelmanganu. The scale of the work is similar to that of rock paintings of Wandjina. Mingelmanganu's stated ambition was to continue cultural practices and religious beliefs through his work; he saw his paintings as perpetuating the power of the Wandjina in the same fashion as do regular restorations of rock paintings. Typical of the full-length figures of Wandjina, the body of Mingelmanganu's image is decorated in lines of dots similar to body–painting designs. They are intended to give the image a visual brightness which expresses the spiritual essence of the ancestral being.

160

138 Pearlshell pendant collected in the 1930s

139 Pearlshell pendant depicting Min-nimb the whale, 1988

The associations of the Wandjina with water, rain and the flashing of lightning, and consequently with the Rainbow Serpent, are also those of the highly prized pearlshell pendants from the western Kimberley. The coastal area around Broome is the source of decorated pearlshells which form a distinctive pictorial tradition in the art of Aboriginal Australia. The antiquity of both undecorated and engraved pearlshells has not been determined, but their production predates the arrival of Europeans. The introduction of metal tools and the arrival of the pearling industry in the latter part of the nineteenth century led to the proliferation of decorated pearlshells from about 1900.

138–9

Pearlshells are used in a number of ways: for rain-making and magical purposes, for trade, in ceremonies, and as personal adornment, when they are worn attached by belts or necklaces of hairstring. Their lustrous quality evokes supernatural power and wellbeing, and equates with the aesthetic of shimmer and brilliance

161

found in painting in Arnhem Land and in the desert. Both decorated and undecorated pearlshells are objects of great value, and are exchanged along trade routes over vast areas of the continent, appearing as far afield as Balgo and Yuendumu in the desert, Roper River in south-east Arnhem Land, Queensland and South Australia.

Historically, pearlshells have often been engraved at the point where they originated, introducing a number of local styles of decoration into the art form. In the Kimberley the designs of pearlshell fall into two general categories, the figurative and the geometric. The latter type encompasses a number of recognizable varieties, including parallel zig-zags, meanders and interlocking key designs. The meanings of the geometric designs are rarely known, although when interpreted they usually indicate manifestations of water in its varied forms, including rain clouds, tidal movements and associated Lightning Snakes.

138   The early pearlshell pendant illustrated was collected in the 1930s and shows a variation on the interlocking key pattern. Typically the engraved lines will be filled with fat and red ochre or, as in this example, powdered charcoal, to highlight the design by giving it the appearance of an inlay. By and large, the production of decorated pearlshells for traditional use had ceased by 1970, although a collection was made for sale by young Bardi and Nyul Nyul men in 139   1988. The example shown carries a highly stylized image of a whale. Plain shells continue to be circulated inland, and old decorated shells are still highly valued. Plain shells will sometimes be incised at centres far removed from their points of origin.

Figurative sculpture has seldom appeared in the Kimberley, although wooden sculptures are known from Wyndham and Kalumburu, towards the east, and clay figures from Halls Creek. In the 1960s a Karajarri artist, John Dodo from La Grange, south of Broome, was commissioned by an elder to carve two wooden figures of the *rayi* (spirit) Walkarurra for a ceremony. Dodo continued to carve figures, and eventually began to sculpt heads in wood, clay and 140   stone. He influenced a number of other artists to take up stone sculpture. Prior to this Dodo had engraved fine wooden ceremonial objects and pearlshells.

Dodo's sandstone sculptures relate directly to the Dreaming in two essential ways: the subjects are ancestral figures, and the stone that he carves was created through an epic ancestral event that occurred near Eighty Mile Beach, south of Broome. The Dreaming relates how a boy broke the law by eating the eggs of a goanna he had killed. This

162

140 John Dodo, *Kungolo*, 1987

act enraged Pulanj, the Rainbow Serpent, who attempted to swallow the boy. Pulanj sent down rain and thunder, and the boy and his family took shelter in a mountain cave. After they had succeeded in blocking the mouth of the cave, the Serpent in his anger began to destroy the mountain, but eventually he gave up and departed. When the storm eased, the family emerged cautiously to find the ground strewn with pieces of rock from the mountain.

REVIVAL IN THE EASTERN KIMBERLEY: THE WARMUN COMMUNITY

There is no dividing line to separate the eastern Kimberley from the west. Given the historical movement of people throughout the region, the art of the east is part of the continuum of Kimberley art, associated with the Wandjina, but also with strong ties to Balgo in the desert, and through the Victoria River Downs area, into Wadeye and Kimul in the Northern Territory.

The last two decades have seen a flourishing of artistic activity in the eastern Kimberley, the focus of which has been the community of

Warmun at Turkey Creek. As at Papunya and elsewhere, events in the region show a contemporary development in Aboriginal art which is founded within traditional idioms.

The early 1970s were unsettling years. Amidst the social upheavals caused by the forced migration of peoples, Aboriginal elders were concerned that the younger generation was forfeiting its culture and law. On Christmas Day 1974, tropical cyclone Tracy destroyed Darwin, the capital city of the Northern Territory. An interpretation of this catastrophic event was revealed in a dream visitation to an elder at Kalumburu; the cyclone was a manifestation of a Rainbow Serpent who had destroyed Darwin, the main centre of European influence in the north of Australia, as a warning to all Aboriginal people to uphold their culture.

In the dream, the elder had revealed to him the songs and dances of a *palga*, or narrative dance cycle, concerning the cyclone. The *palga* provides a vehicle by which the interpretation of such events can be revealed to the general public. The ceremonies that ensued were the beginning of a renascence of ritual activity and cultural affirmation across the Kimberley. For these ceremonies, constructions incorporating emblems or painted boards and structures of coloured threaded string or wool, commonly known as thread-crosses, are made and carried behind the performers' heads. Most prominent are the boards painted with a conventionalized image of the cyclone near Darwin, and a long thread-cross of the associated Wandjina in serpent form.

During the same period a Kukatja/Wangkajunga man at Warmun, Rover Thomas, had a visitation from the spirit of a female relative who had died, after a car crash, in an aeroplane taking her to hospital in Perth. At the moment of her death the aeroplane was over a whirlpool out at sea, in the Indian Ocean off Derby. The whirlpool is the home of another Rainbow Serpent, Juntarkal, who named sacred sites and gave people language right across the eastern Kimberley. The stories of the travels of the spirit of the deceased woman from the whirlpool to her conception-site near Turkey Creek were revealed to Thomas in the form of songs and dances, a new *palga*, called the Kuril Kuril (pronounced 'grill grill'). The spirit of the woman was accompanied by another being called Tjimpi, the spirit of a long-deceased woman. The Kuril Kuril painted boards carried images of Darwin and the cyclone, as well as of ancestral beings and places the two female spirits encountered on their journey.

As the owner of the ceremony, Rover Thomas did not paint any of the early boards, but instructed others, principally his mother's

141 Paddy Jaminji, *Manginta the Devil Devil*, c. 1977, from the *Kuril Kuril* ceremonial series

brother, Paddy Jaminji. *Manginta the Devil Devil* was one of the   141
boards used in the first Kuril Kuril. At a place that bears its name,
Manginta replaced Tjimpi as the companion of the woman's spirit on
the journey. The connection between spirit and place is expressed in
the painting, which represents the horned head of Manginta while
simultaneously suggesting the landscape, seen in plan view as a
combination of conventional symbols. This visual duality is a
characteristic of the art of the eastern Kimberley.

In the early 1980s, outside interest in the emblems used in the public
ceremony encouraged artists to paint boards of subjects related to the   143
Kuril Kuril and other themes, not for ceremonial use but for sale. As
they were not to be carried in the *palga* the size of these paintings
increased, and in 1986 the Warmun artists were introduced to canvas
as a substitute for the original wooden boards. In the early paintings,
the Kuril Kuril *palga* provided the context in which the images
operated, consequently the boards usually contained single images
against monochrome red or black grounds. As paintings were made
for sale, the images have become more complex, and the context in   144
which the icons operate is provided by the painting and its associated
text or story.

142 Rover Thomas, *Cyclone Tracy*, 1991

142   The subject of *Cyclone Tracy* by Rover Thomas recalls the origins
of the Kuril Kuril ceremony. The black form represents the cyclone
gathering intensity as it heads towards Darwin. The shape relates to
conventional images of the subject developed in early dance emblems.
Minor winds are shown as forms emanating from the main image.

Rover Thomas began painting Kuril Kuril emblems in 1981, and
over the next decade pursued a vigorous and prolific artistic life which
led to his selection in 1990 as one of the first two Aboriginal artists to
represent Australia at the Venice Biennale (the other being Trevor
Nickolls). Thomas has elaborated on the pictorial conventions of the
region to articulate a highly personal vision. He introduces an
interplay between broad areas of natural colour, unfaltering line, bold
forms, and uncompromising composition. In his paintings, the land
becomes an allegory for ancestral dramas, personal experiences and
historical events.

143 Jock Mosquito
Jubarljari, *Kawarrin*,
1984

144 Jack Britten,
*Purnululu (Bull Creek
country)*, 1988

145 George Mung
Mung, *Binoowoon
country*, 1990

145 The paintings by artists from Warmun display some of the elements of the art of the desert, in particular the use of concentric designs such as circles to denote specific sites, lines of dots to describe shapes, and a planar view of the landscape. Among Warmun artists, however, the emphasis is on the depiction of the features of the environment created by the ancestors, rather than on the narration of ancestral events, as in desert painting.

143 Jock Mosquito Jubarljari's *Kawarrin* on the Kuril Kuril trail, for example, depicts the hills in profile as rows of arches, and sites as linked sets of concentric circles. The setting for Jack Britten's

144 *Purnululu (Bull Creek country)* is the spectacular sandstone canyons of the Purnululu or Bungle Bungle ranges near Turkey Creek, the site of an encounter between two spirit beings. The hills and valleys of Purnululu are depicted in profile. The alternating rows of dots and lines echo the striated surfaces of the cliff-faces while also referring to ceremonial body-designs. These lines are incised into the surface of the painting in a zig-zagging motion, a technique similar to one used

138 to engrave boab nuts and pearlshell pendants.

145 The simultaneous use of different perspectives of the land is evident in *Binoowoon country* by George Mung Mung. The meandering black line at the right of the painting defines the high hill surrounding the valley of Gandawarranginy in Binoowoon country, south of Turkey Creek. This is where the ancestral Crocodile walked in the Dreaming. Trees are shown in profile, oriented towards an area of flat, undecorated ground and the dominant curved shape of a site called Garnawoony, associated with a toxic yam. In contrast, the black shapes indicating an area of rocky hills to the left offer a profile view of the landscape.

The art of the Kimberley, as seen through the artists mentioned here, is marked by a range of idioms and influences. The traditions of the Wandjina continue to pervade much of the area, while the Walmajarri and other desert people have introduced their own artistic styles. In a few years, the artists of Warmun fostered a school of painting begun in response to the need of Aboriginal people in the Kimberley to strengthen their culture in the face of adversity. Cultural renewal is marked by artistic activity throughout the Kimberley. Within the diverse artistic practices that make up the art of the region, a number of artists have developed distinctively individual approaches, Jarinyanu David Downs, Jimmy Pike, John Dodo and Rover Thomas among them.

CHAPTER FIVE

Diversity: North Queensland and the Torres Strait Islands

The art of the northern part of Queensland, including that of the peoples of Cape York Peninsula, Mornington Island and the Torres 3
Strait Islands, represents a number of distinct traditions, each of which today incorporates many innovations. Culturally and historically, the region is not homogeneous. In parts of the Cape, Aboriginal people have maintained traditional links with their ancestral lands, while the people of the Torres Strait Islands have cultural affiliations with Papua New Guinea and their art traditions are distinctive. As a consequence, the region is characterized by a diversity of art styles, influences and practices.

A UNIFYING ART: CAPE YORK PENINSULA

The most enduring form of art in northern Queensland is found at Cape York Peninsula in the spectacular galleries of paintings and engravings on the rock walls and caves of the Laura district, north of 146

146 Paintings on rock wall in the Emu Gallery, Laura, Queensland

147 Unknown artist, shield, collected 1897

148 Unknown artist, basket, nineteenth century

Cairns. Engravings here have been dated to fifteen thousand years ago. The rainforest regions along the eastern coast are renowned for a range of painted clubs, throwing sticks, paddles, shields and weavings. 146 In contrast to the figurative and often schematic images of Laura rock art, these objects are characterized by bold geometric or conventionalized designs, although some naturalistic images do appear.

Among the best-known rainforest art forms, perhaps because their broad, flat decorated surfaces are readily equated with European 147 notions of painting, are men's fighting shields, used in initiation ceremonies and in battle, when the painted designs were intended to embody protective qualities. The range and variety of these conventionalized, often symmetrical designs suggest a highly developed visual language. The significance of these designs is not well known; however, a number have been described as denoting totemic species as well as objects such as boomerangs and carrying-bags. The 148 same is true of the distinctive horned baskets woven from strips of lawyer-cane and painted with earth-pigments. The works shown were collected at the end of the nineteenth century from the Cardwell district near Cairns. In recent years, artists in the region have revived

170

techniques and forms as part of a movement towards cultural renewal.

In the early 1950s boldly painted figurative sculpture emerged from Aurukun on the west coast of the Cape. Although simple sculptural forms from earlier times are known, the recent works are often composite in nature. They are usually painted in broad areas of colour, similar to ceremonial body-decorations, and represent ancestral beings in human and animal form. The sculptures are the foci around which ceremonial narrative dances are performed. The sculptural tradition continues today but it is generally restricted to ceremonial objects. Only a few sculptures have been made for sale outside the community.

While most Aurukun sculpture is overtly naturalistic, conventional forms do exist. *Flying foxes* by Arthur Koo'ekka Pambegan senior and his son of the same name is a public sculpture that was used in a ceremony. The sculpture concerns two ancestral Flying Fox Men who broke the law by killing their own totem, the flying fox. The event is part of a saga about the continuous bickering and fighting among Flying Fox ancestors. The Men tied the flying foxes to a pole and attempted to cook them. In the sculpture, the long sticks represent black flying foxes and the short sticks are red flying foxes. The arrangement of this sculpture, two forked sticks supporting a horizontal bar, is similar in form to the bark huts and ceremonial structures used in the region and in Arnhem Land. 149

149 Arthur Koo'ekka Pambegan senior and Arthur Koo'ekka Pambegan junior, *Flying foxes*, 1962

150 Angus Namponan with Nelson Wolmby and Peter Peemuggina, *Two Young Women of Cape Keerweer*, 1987

150   *Two Young Women of Cape Keerweer* points to the contemporary relevance of religion, ceremony and art in Aboriginal society. The sculpture was made for a ritual to release the spirit of a young man who died in the Aurukun jail. The subject of the sculpture is two young Quail Women from different clans who were caring for a sick child. The women sat on their adjacent clan lands and each sang mourning songs which the other admired. The child died but its relatives, all Bird Ancestors in human form, refused to grieve for it. The women crossed an estuary and met at the boundary between their clan estates, where they sank into a cave and became sharks, causing the murky waters of the estuary to clear. The child's relatives were transformed into bird beings.

    The dotted body-painting design on the sculpture reflects the sparkle of the clear waters of the estuary after the monsoon season and, as in desert art and the *rarrk* of Arnhem Land, the dots impart a notion of brilliance and the presence of supernatural power. In combination with the physical attributes of the women the dots signify health, beauty and fertility.

The particular significance of the sculpture lies in the fact that the Quail Women belonged to the Wik-Ngatharr and Wik-Ngathan clans, as did the parents of the man for whose spirit the ceremony was performed. The three artists who made the work in collaboration also belong to these clans, Angus Namponan to the Wik-Ngatharr clan and his assistants Nelson Wolmby and Peter Peemuggina to the Wik-Ngathan. By the collaborative nature of their work they reinforce the theme of social cohesion at a time of communal unrest expressed by the story of the Quail Women.

To the north of Aurukun, the town of Weipa is the birthplace of Thancoupie, one of Australia's leading ceramicists, and one of the first contemporary Aboriginal artists to be recognized in the international art world. While Thancoupie draws inspiration from the traditions of her people, the Thanaquith, she has developed a vehicle for personal artistic expression in her ceramics. There is no history of pottery in traditional Aboriginal society, although clay has a significant role in ceremonial activity and in art. The Thanaquith traditionally baked clay balls which were stored to make paint for use in rituals. Their affinity with clay has been translated into Thancoupie's spherical pots which are symbolic of unity, fire and mother earth, and are decorated with images from traditional stories.

151

151 Thancoupie, *Garth Eran and Evarth Eran*, 1988

152 Goobalathaldin (Dick Roughsey), *Rainbow Serpent, Thwaithu dance,*
Mornington Island, 1972

NARRATIVE ART: MORNINGTON ISLAND

3   The Lardil people on Mornington Island, in the south-eastern basin of
the Gulf of Carpentaria, have associations with Aurukun to the east
and with Groote Eylandt in the west. Since the 1950s bark painting
has become a feature of Mornington Island art, showing some
60   connections in style with the bark painting of Groote Eylandt. The
152   most prominent painter from Mornington Island was Goobalathaldin
(Dick Roughsey), who worked in a number of media and also
illustrated several children's books of ancestral stories.

    The narrative nature of Mornington Island bark painting appears in
153   *Two stories* by Kirk A. Watt, one of the current generation of artists.
Watt depicts, in the upper panel, the Whirlwind Man chasing a Brolga
(Crane) Woman he intends to marry. She adopts the form of the bird,
and flees. In the lower section, a Turtle Boy who has broken the law

174

153 Kirk A. Watt, *Two stories*, 1991

and run away from his people is depicted diving into the water. By singing, he transforms himself into a turtle and makes good his escape. In the centre of the painting, three Lardil people are fishing with spears and traps. The painting concerns metamorphosis, the great spiritual theme common throughout Aboriginal Australia. In the case of the Turtle Boy, the metaphor of entering and emerging to effect the transformation is expressed through the image of the hollow log.

The figures here are rendered naturalistically and set against a decorated ground of dots, although patterns of dashes, similar to those in recent Groote Eylandt paintings, are also found in Mornington Island bark paintings. The use of dots in *Two stories* links the work with the art of Aurukun, while the division of the painting into panels and the centrally placed waterhole reflect the influence of Arnhem Land. The work also displays a degree of innovation in the treatment of the figures; they are highly animated with details of physical features, and several figures are shown in profile with an indication of perspective in the European sense.

MOVING IMAGES: TORRES STRAIT ISLAND ART

3   The more-than-one-hundred islands of the Torres Strait, of which only a few are permanently inhabited, once formed a land bridge between Aboriginal Cape York and Papua New Guinea. While Island culture bears affinities with both Papuan and Aboriginal cultures, it is distinct from either. Today many Islanders live on the mainland, in northern Queensland, but social contacts with Papua are maintained. Contact with Europeans was intermittent until the London Missionary Society established itself on Erub (Darnley Island) in 1871, heralding the spread of European influence throughout the islands. Over the decades the cumulative effect of missionary prohibitions and colonial rule disrupted, but did not eradicate traditional practices. In recent years Islanders have had some of their ownership rights to land recognized, and a process of cultural renewal is developing.

In common with Aboriginal Australians, the Islanders' cultural history is primarily transmitted orally and through ceremonies which provide the stimulus for the production of many of the plastic arts. Among the ritual accoutrements are masks, articulated headdresses and dance accessories, drums and woven items. In the eastern islands elaborately carved and incised turtleshell once formed the basis for spectacular dance masks. Turtleshell masks were observed by the

154 *Krar* (mask), nineteenth century

155 Ken Thaiday, *Beizam (shark) dance mask*, 1991

explorer Torres in 1660. Nearly four centuries later the drums and masks of the Torres Straits were the first types of Australian plastic arts 154 to make an impact on the artists of the Surrealist movement in Paris.

The tradition of mask-making for ceremony continues today with artists adopting modern materials in their construction. Ken Thaiday 155 from Erub constructs headdresses and hand-held 'dance-machines' for use in public ceremonies. As with their forerunners, Thaiday's constructions are articulated to enable the dancer to move parts of the mask during the performance. *Beizam (shark) dance mask* is constructed of plastic and plywood, showing the jaws and teeth of a shark which hide the wearer's face. The menacing presence of the shark, a symbol of law and order, is mitigated by the rows of feathers attached to the jaws. In the upper half of the mask is the figure of a hammer-head shark, which can also be manipulated by the wearer.

156 Jenuarrie, *Our time has begun*, 1986

In 1984 the opportunities for Islander and Aboriginal people of the region to develop their art were enhanced by the establishment of an art school in Cairns, dedicated to their needs. The school was set up by European art teachers, although the prominent Aboriginal potter Thancoupie was one of the original instructors. Students are encouraged to work in a variety of media and to draw on their local traditions; for example, Jenuarrie's batik *Our time has begun* is influenced by the Quinkan figures found in the rock art of the Laura district.

151

156

Although they live in a city outside their traditional areas, the students at Cairns have played an important role in the revival of art among Aboriginal and Torres Strait Islander people in the north of Queensland. Their work is attracting much attention, as indeed is that of urban and rural Aboriginal artists throughout Australia.

178

CHAPTER SIX

Artists in the town and city

Aboriginal people living outside traditional environments have played a significant role in the renascence of Aboriginal culture in the second half of the twentieth century. The period has witnessed the rise to prominence of artists from urban and rural backgrounds whose links to their cultural heritages have been, to varying degrees, severed by the impact of colonization and decades of official policies of family separation and assimilation. While their art proclaims their Aboriginal identity, it often operates beyond the classical idioms. It does not conform to one style, but draws inspiration from Aboriginal practices and European techniques alike. This art reflects a unique perspective born of a distinctive experience.

Such urban and rural Aboriginal artists have been seen as on the periphery of artistic practice in Australia. When seeking to accept Aboriginal art, Australian society at large perceived traditional forms alone as the authentic expression of Aboriginality. At the beginning of the century, for example, the value of the *toas* (pp. 101–2) was considered to lie in their antiquity as forms of Diyari art. The first acrylic paintings from Papunya were regarded in many quarters with suspicion. Authenticity was equated with tradition, and the value of the object lay in its expression of a time and culture gone by rather than in its relevance as a reflection of contemporary circumstances. As a consequence, urban and rural artists who did not fit into any preconceived categories were denied the opportunities open to other Australian artists, and their work was largely ignored.

The phrases 'urban' and 'rural' Aboriginal are generally used to refer to artists who prefer to describe themselves by local generic words for Aboriginal, the most common of which are 'Nyoongah' in south-western Australia, 'Nunga' in coastal South Australia, 'Murri' in the north-east and 'Koori' in the south-east. In addition, artists often identify their particular language group to establish their cultural identity. The descriptions 'urban' and 'rural' are, at best, useful terms to denote, not a style of art, but the social milieu of the artists.

3

157 William Barak, *Corroboree, c.* 1885

The political and social breakthroughs of the 1960s and 1970s saw the end of the policy of assimilation of Aboriginal people into the dominant European culture, and laid the groundwork for the official recognition of Aboriginal culture. The emergence of urban and rural art has been part of this process of change. The origins of such art, however, can be found in the nineteenth century.

Some of the precursors of today's urban and rural artists emerged from the south-eastern corner of the continent where the first impact of European colonization was keenly felt. South-eastern Australia, as other areas, has a rich heritage of traditional art forms, many of which are common to most of Aboriginal Australia, though some types are peculiar to the area. The carving of trees as grave or ceremonial-ground markers in New South Wales and the making of mantles from decorated possum skins are distinctive practices. Besides rock engraving and painting, body painting and ground painting in ceremony, painting or drawing on bark is also known, although only two barks from mid-nineteenth-century Victoria survive. Of these,

4, 9

one from near Lake Tyrrell, made in the 1860s, is executed in a naturalistic fashion to show scenes of hunting and fishing, a ceremony or fight, and a squatter's house as evidence of European presence.

In the mid-nineteenth century, new forms of Aboriginal art began to develop at the interface of Aboriginal and European cultures. The tradition of drawing as seen on bark and rock continued in the work of a number of artists using the introduced materials of ink, pencil, paper and board. William Barak and Tommy McRae, the best known of several artists working at the time, produced drawings which were commissioned from them by European settlers.

William Barak was an elder of the Woiwurrung people who lived on the site of the present city of Melbourne. When, in 1863, the Woiwurrung were resettled at nearby Coranderrk, Barak began to draw images primarily of ceremonial life. *Corroboree* depicts a ritual 157 where figures draped in possum-skin mantles are formally arranged in rows. Barak's concern with naturalistic representation appears secondary to the expression of the organized relationships between the participants in the ceremony, reflecting relationships on the social and religious scale.

Tommy McRae lived on the upper Murray River in northern Victoria, and from the 1860s on, he found a number of patrons who

158 Tommy McRae, page from a sketchbook of *c.* 1890

supplied him with the materials to draw scenes of hunting, fishing and ceremonies, as well as other images of contemporary life. McRae's work was well-regarded, and examples were used to illustrate two volumes of Aboriginal stories published in 1896 and 1898. McRae imbued his thin silhouetted figures with individual character and expression. The arrangement of the figures in a page from his *c.* 1890 sketchbook shows dancers accompanied by an orchestra which includes a Chinese fiddle-player and a drummer. The composition diverges from the formality of Barak's ceremonial image, and indeed from McRae's own drawings of rituals. In this drawing, apart from their clothing and the musical instruments, the jaunty postures of the figures and their loose alignment in rows suggests a scene of revelry rather than ritual.

158

The fact that Aboriginal artists such as Barak and McRae were commissioned by and sold their work to Europeans is significant in the history of relations between the two groups. Despite the prevailing attitudes towards Aboriginal people, these artists could command a place in the new environment. In addition, their work provides rare Aboriginal commentaries on nineteenth-century life in the rapidly changing Australia. Their art embodies cultural ideals and perspectives which are an important part of the heritage of late twentieth-century urban and rural artists.

The art establishment in the first half of the twentieth century was still concerned with European models from the previous century, and virtually ignored the revolutionary developments in Western art. While the Cubists, Surrealists, Dadaists and others found avenues for release from the tired artistic structures of Europe in the forms of African, indigenous American and Oceanic art, Australians were more interested in the official art of the Salon. With a few exceptions, the work of Aboriginal artists living in the urban and rural areas who continued to elaborate on traditional techniques such as weavings and decorated boomerangs was regarded by the Australian art world as a manifestation of a degenerate tradition, or as kitsch. Despite this, the persistence of art practices among urban and rural people has proved significant in the flowering of art in the late twentieth century.

89

The popularity of the work of Albert Namatjira in the 1950s was a source of inspiration to urban and rural artists, who sought role models where these were sadly lacking. Ronald Bull (1942–79) from Melbourne and Revel Cooper (1933–83) from the Aboriginal settlement at Carrolup, outside Perth, both regarded as painters in the European landscape tradition, gained a degree of recognition in their

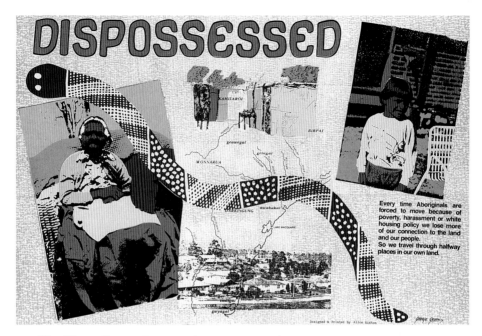

"Every time Aboriginals are forced to move because of poverty, harassment or white housing policy we lose more of our connection to the land and our people. So we travel through halfway places in our own land."

159 Alice Hinton-Bateup, *Dispossessed*, 1986

lifetimes, and showed the potential for urban artists to break through the barriers of prejudice.

THE FIRST WAVE

In the second half of the twentieth century, as the movements for the recognition of Aboriginal rights gained momentum, urban and rural artists found compelling reasons to produce art. Aboriginal people required imagery and symbols with which to express their ideals and aspirations. The issues of dispossession, broken families, racism – the secret history of Australia – and an intensification of the sense of cultural identity provided strong motivation, and these themes are all part of the repertoire of artists.

The 1970s was also a period of change in Australian culture generally and in Australian art in particular. New government initiatives promoted the arts and offered financial and practical support for a greater number of artists. A broadening of the concept of what constituted art saw an explosion of activity in areas previously deemed the lesser arts. Ephemeral arts such as performance art and the

183

multiple forms of photography and printmaking became popular vehicles for expression because of their potential to reach wide audiences.

The print, as a relatively simple and inexpensive way of creating multiple images, became an attractive medium for urban artists. The era saw the establishment of community print workshops across the country to which Aboriginal artists had access. Avril Quaill produced the screenprinted poster *Trespassers keep out* at the Earthworks Poster Collective in Sydney. Quaill's image is based on the unifying symbol of Aboriginal Australia, the Aboriginal flag, designed in 1971 by the artist Harold Thomas (born 1947). In the circle of the yellow sun of the flag, an old Aboriginal man crouches defiantly against a typical white Australian suburban picket fence bearing the ironic admonition of the title.

Alice Hinton-Bateup, working through the Garage Graphix print workshop in Sydney, combines words and imagery to express a sense of loss of heritage and a call for social justice. *Dispossessed* is another poster boldly revealing the plight of Aboriginal people and

160 Kevin Gilbert, *My father's studio*, 1965, reprinted 1990

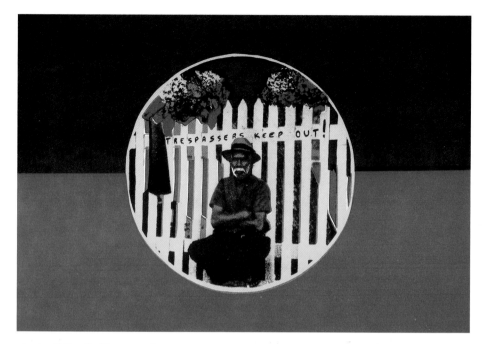

161 Avril Quaill, *Trespassers keep out*, 1982

proclaiming Aboriginal ties to the land. The text speaks of the institutionalized movement of Aboriginal people for reasons of 'poverty, harassment or white housing policy'.

The first Koori printmaker, Kevin Gilbert, began working in the   160
period before the establishment of widely accessible facilities, and before Aboriginal art generally had made an impact on the consciousness of the Australian public. Gilbert, a Wiradjuri poet, playwright, social activist and artist, produced a set of linocuts between 1965 and 1969 which were reprinted in 1990. As in his writings, the subjects concern the maintenance of traditional values in the quest for social justice and equality in modern Australia.

In the 1970s Thancoupie and the painter Trevor Nickolls were pioneers in establishing a place on the Australian scene for artists working outside the classical Aboriginal traditions. Their achievements opened the way for others to follow.

Nickolls had been an art student in Adelaide, and while he cared   163
little for the institutionalization of art, he accumulated a wealth of influences as diverse as Giotto, Cubism and Surrealism at a time when

185

Hard-edge abstraction held sway in Australian art. However, Nickolls chose his Aboriginality as his main subject, and he set about expressing in paint the dilemmas facing the individual caught between two cultures and isolated from both. Alienation is the theme of the *Dreamtime/Machinetime* series of paintings, begun in the period 1978 to 1981, in which Nickolls developed a personal lexicon of imagery. The turning point in Nickolls's career came in 1979 when he became acquainted with the Warlpiri artist Dinny Nolan Tjampit-jinpa. Through Nolan, Nickolls learnt about desert painting. In 1981 Nickolls went to live in Darwin where he could experience at first hand the art of Arnhem Land. As he became familiar with traditional art practices, Nickolls found inspiration in the formal elements of classical Aboriginal painting.

163   By the time he painted *Waterhole and trees* in 1986, Nickolls had moved back south to Sydney. Although more strident images were to follow, the work embodies a reconciliation of stylistic influences; it pays homage to the classical Aboriginal idioms while reinforcing the artist's personal vision. The painting depicts a formally arranged landscape with the waterhole at the centre and four trees arranged symmetrically around it. The ground is made of clusters of coloured dots which flatten the landscape against the picture plane in a manner reminiscent of the planar view of the landscape in desert painting. However, the perfectly circular waterhole is seen in perspective as an ellipse, and the trees cast shadows indicating the three-dimensional nature of the space. The pictorial depth of the image is emphasized by the boomerang-shape and the shadow it casts which continues beyond the picture frame.

Nickolls was one of nearly thirty artists represented in *Koori Art '84* at the Contemporary Art Space in Sydney, a watershed exhibition for urban Aboriginal art and artists. The show articulated the concerns of Aboriginal artists working outside the traditional Aboriginal frame-work, but also included non-urban artists using European media and techniques: Banduk Marika's prints, Turkey Tolson Tjupurrula's and Johnny Warrangula Tjupurrula's experiments with landscapes in the European manner, Ernabella batik and contemporary watercolours from Hermannsburg, among others.

Koori Art '84 also brought together several artists who had been working in isolation yet had much in common. All lacked opportunities to have their work seen and shared similar aspirations. From the exhibition developed the Boomalli Aboriginal Artists Cooperative, formed in 1987 by Sydney-based artists to provide

162 James Simon, *Reflected images of heaven and earth*, 1991

studio and exhibition spaces as well as to promote the work of its members.

Institutional acceptance of the work of Koori artists began. One work in *Koori Art '84*, Jeffrey Samuels's *This changing continent of Australia*, was acquired by the Art Gallery of New South Wales. The painting, composed of repeated silhouettes of the continent of Australia, reflects the traditional Aboriginal theme of identification with and definition of one's own land. It heralded a new age for urban artists across Australia. 164

References to traditional artistic practices have recurred in the work of urban artists. The highly animated and intricately detailed surfaces of classical Aboriginal painting, for instance, find an echo in *Reflected images of heaven and earth* by James Simon, another of the artists represented in the ground-breaking exhibition of 1984. 162

The work of two photographers Brenda Croft and Michael Riley (now film-maker) presents a powerful alternative to the negative stereotypes of Aboriginal people seen in popular imagery and in the daily press. Riley's portraits of Aboriginal people such as *Christina* 165

163 Trevor Nickolls, *Waterhole and trees*, 1986

emphasize the beauty and dignity of individuals, as opposed to the voyeuristic and anonymous images which proliferate in the public domain. Croft records the Aboriginal struggle from the perspective of the Aboriginal as hero, rather than villain as usually portrayed in the popular media. The defiant figure of *Michael Watson* sports a shirt which ridicules the claiming of Australia for the British by the sea captain James Cook in 1770. The occasion of Croft's photograph was another significant moment in the Aboriginal political struggle – when Aboriginal people from all over Australia gathered in Sydney in a demonstration of cultural strength on the day Australia was celebrating two hundred years of European colonization.

166

Fiona Foley seeks inspiration within the traditional cultural setting, in particular from the culture of her own people, the Badtjala from Fraser Island in Queensland. *Annihilation of the blacks* is a potent allegory of the treatment of Aboriginal people at the hands of the colonizers; a white figure stands watch over a group of hanging black figures. The structure of the work reflects classical ceremonial sculptural forms such as the *Flying foxes* from Aurukun.

167

149

188

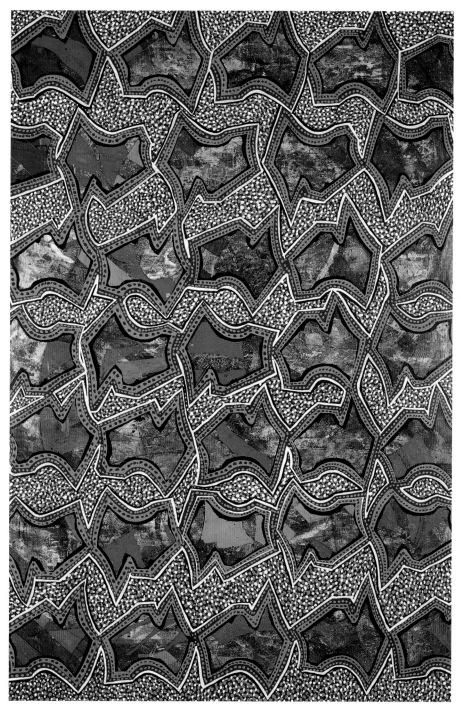

164 Jeffrey Samuels, *This changing continent of Australia*, 1984

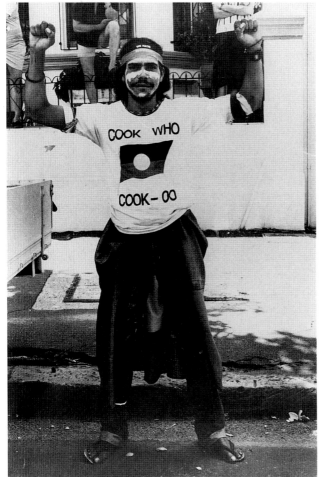

165 Michael Riley, *Christina*, 1986

166 Brenda Croft, *Michael Watson in Redfern on the Long March of Freedom, Justice and Hope, Invasion Day, 26 January 1988, Sydney, NSW*, 1988

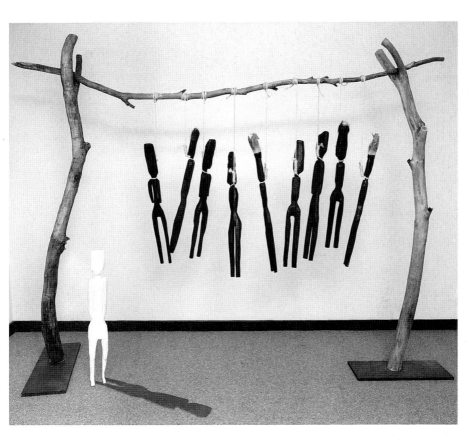

167 Fiona Foley, *Annihilation of the blacks*, 1986

168 Lin Onus, *Dingoes; dingo proof fence*, 1989, detail from the series *Dingoes*

169 (*left*) Euphemia Bostock, *Possum skin print*, 1990

170 (*above*) Bluey Roberts, *River spirit*, 1992

OPPOSITE

171 (*above*) Sally Morgan, *Moon and stars*, 1987

172 (*below*) Bronwyn Bancroft, *Cycle of life cape*, 1987

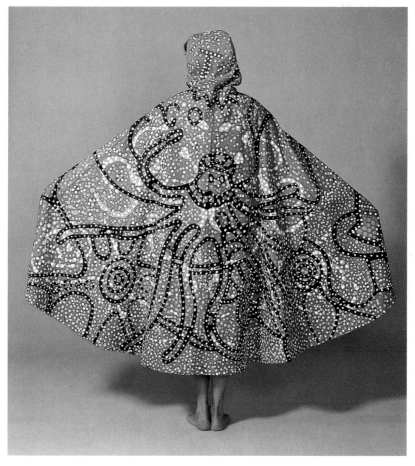

The paintings and sculptures of Lin Onus are executed in a hyper-real manner to juxtapose images drawn from Aboriginal Australia with those of western culture. Onus, like Foley, has sought direct exchange with artists living in traditional communities, and is now one of several artists who make pilgrimages to Arnhem Land and 168 other art provinces. Onus's installation *Dingoes* consists of sets of fibreglass dogs painted in stripes of red, yellow, black and white, the four basic Aboriginal colours. The sculpture is a sympathetic but ironic comment on popular perceptions of a much-maligned indigenous dog: the word 'dingo' has entered non-Aboriginal Australian parlance to mean a despicable person or a coward. In one detail, the spirit-dog breaches the dingo fence which runs across thousands of kilometres of the country to protect introduced grazing-animals, cattle and sheep, and serves as a metaphor for the treatment of Aboriginal people.

The first wave of urban artists work in a variety of media. Bluey Roberts continues the tradition of decorating boomerangs in highly innovative ways. His work includes engraving the multi-layered 170, 169 shells of emu eggs. Euphemia Bostock's fabric length *Possum skin print* translates images based on decorations found on possum-skin mantles, once common in the south-east of the country, on to fabric that is also

173 Arone Raymond Meeks, *Healing place*, 1988

Within the image (handwritten and printed text): With pride, my children will use the names of our ancestors. 'Nyoongar' 'Njamanji' FELLOW AUSTRALIAN

174 Byron Pickett, *Fellow Australian*, 1985

intended to be worn. Bronwyn Bancroft's design in the hand-painted *Cycle of life cape* takes the form of a narrative describing the procreative journey of an Aboriginal couple. The concern to continue traditional narratives through images is evident in the work of a number of urban artists, including Arone Raymond Meeks' lithograph *Healing place*.   172

   173

Byron Pickett and Sally Morgan were among a group of Nyoongah artists from Western Australia to make an impact in the art world at the same time as their counterparts on the east coast. Sally Morgan's colour screenprint *Moon and stars* relates to traditional beliefs and includes the image of the Rainbow Snake. In other works, Morgan explores her family's history of survival in an often antagonistic and threatening society. Byron Pickett's *Fellow Australian* expresses the sense of pride in Aboriginal culture and its continuity. It also appeals for the equal treatment of Aboriginal people. The quest for equality and justice within Australian society as a whole has been a resonant and recurring theme in the work of the first wave of urban Aboriginal artists.   171

   174

175 (overleaf) Ramingining artists, *The Aboriginal Memorial* (detail), 1988 ▶

The pioneering efforts of the first group of urban artists during the 1970s and 1980s created opportunities for urban and rurally based artists and a wider interest in their work. The second wave emerged in the late 1980s, and included Robert Campbell junior, whose stated ambition as a painter had been to record Aboriginal history for his family. By 1987 his work was receiving wider scrutiny. Campbell works in the manner of a social commentator, depicting episodes of Australian history as seen from the Aboriginal perspective. His art deals with a wide range of subjects, from pre-European Aboriginal life to commentaries on racism through images of segregated picture-theatres and whites-only swimming pools.

176   Campbell also documents significant moments in Aboriginal history. *Aboriginal embassy* was painted fourteen years after the dramatic events which forged a change in official attitudes to Aboriginal land rights. A tent embassy had been set up outside the federal parliament building in Canberra in 1972 to highlight the dispossession of Aboriginal people and the denial of sovereign rights to their land. The painting displays the characteristics of Campbell's

176   Robert Campbell junior, *Aboriginal embassy*, 1986

177 Gordon Bennett, *Outsider*, 1988   178 Karen Casey, *Got the bastard*, 1991

work – the sequential narrative and the depiction of the figures, usually naked, to show the oesophagus. The top panel depicts the protagonists and their supporters, who are shown being arrested in the lower section. The intensely rich decoration on each of the elements animates the painting surface and has parallels in the fine engravings on shields, clubs and boomerangs of south-eastern Australia.

The Aboriginal perspective on Australian history and society is also a theme in the work of Gordon Bennett. Bennett's analysis of contemporary Australian culture reveals the extent to which negative stereotyped images of Aboriginal people are used as a vehicle for propaganda and social conditioning. Bennett constantly juxtaposes familiar images of Aboriginal and European Australia to lend them new meanings. *Outsider* is a metaphorical attack on the citadel of European art. The headless Aboriginal figure, in full ceremonial body paint, infiltrates one of the western world's icons, van Gogh's

177

179 Judy Watson, *Heartland*, 1991

Vincent's Bedroom at Arles, 1889. The figure has crashed through the window to stand menacingly over two classical heads lying on van Gogh's bed. Blood spurts into the swirls of van Gogh's *Starry Night* of 1889. Despite the assault, Bennett's admiration for van Gogh's achievement is undisguised.

The writing of history by the dominant culture is a subject of the work of Tasmanian-born Karen Casey. *Got the bastard* depicts a burly 178 hunter with a gloating expression holding a rifle across his lap, while to his right in the dim light hangs the carcass of a Tasmanian tiger, a now-extinct marsupial. The image refers to the systematic hunting down of Tasmanian Aboriginal people in the early part of the nineteenth century, an exercise so effective that the Tasmanian Aboriginal population was believed to have been exterminated by 1876. The placing of the symbol for the oppressed, the tiger, in the half-light of the background suggests that the story of the oppression of Aboriginal people has been deliberately hidden in Australia's official history. *Got the bastard* also has more universal implications, in commenting on the aggressive and wanton destruction of the environment through misunderstanding and ignorance.

In the paintings of Judy Watson, history is embedded in the land which is marked with the evidence of past events. Watson focuses on the processes of art-making in Aboriginal Australia. The concepts linking land, family and history are expressed in her work. Washes of paint and marks in dry pigment combine to produce textures of stone, water and earth, and refer to the presence of her ancestors in the land. Paintings such as *Heartland* are tactile maps of her ancestors' country 179 of north-western Queensland.

The personal life-experiences of rural people provide a rich source of inspiration for artists. Ian W. Abdulla's work records childhood memories of growing up on the fringe of Australian society, in this case in the Coorong on the lower Murray River, near Adelaide. In *Sowing seeds at nite* the tractor lights illuminate the ground, allowing 180 the planting to take place in the cool night air. Abdulla's preoccupation with recording family history is expressed through the combination of image with descriptive text. Ricky Maynard records his people's environment and working life through the camera lens: *Jason Thomas, Terry Maynard and David Maluga* portrays a mutton 183 bird hunt on Flinders Island in Bass Strait. Images such as these express people's pride in their lives and a positive self-image that contradicts common negative stereotypes.

When I was a teenage boy, at Gerard Mission and just started working we were taught how to put a crop in we were getting that good that we used to put in a crop after dark while the weather was cooler.

Ian.W. Abdulla

180 Ian W. Abdulla, *Sowing seeds at nite*, 1990

181 (*below left*) Pooaraar (Bevan Hayward), *Spirits of the Australian bushlands*, 1988

182 (*below right*) Treahna Hamm, *Rebirth II*, 1991

183 (*right*) Ricky Maynard, Jason Thomas, Terry Maynard and David Maluga, 1985

Concern with identity is a recurring theme in urban art. Pooaraar (Bevan Hayward) investigates the dilemma of the individual of both Aboriginal and non-Aboriginal heritage through a series of metaphorical images of the animals and spirit figures that inhabit the Australian bush, as in the linocut *Spirits of the Australian bushlands*. The 181 subject is reinterpreted in imagery symbolic of fertility in *Rebirth II* by 182 Treahna Hamm.

The work of urban and rural artists continues to refer to traditional forms and themes as part of the process of cultural enhancement. Rick Roser's *Jundal gianga (woman powerful)* expresses the fecund power of 184 this ancestor-being, who carries spirit children in her fighting-club leg and a bolt of lightning in her arms as she seeks a father for her children. The sculpture is made from native materials, various woods, cabbage-palm string, emu feathers and ochres, to emphasize links with tradition. In the Coorong, Ngarrindjeri men and women weave coiled bundles of sedge-grass into baskets and other functional items. These techniques are continued today by artists such as Yvonne Koolmatrie, who points to the sculptural qualities of traditional forms in the large *Eel trap*.

In *Crisis: what to do about this half-caste thing*, Richard Bell confronts the issue of racial prejudice in a bold and sardonic manner, with three figures, the black, the white and the harlequin half-caste in the upper central section of the painting. The work focuses on the historical treatment of Aboriginal people, in particular those of 'mixed blood', known by the derogatory term 'half-caste'. The painting juxtaposes symbols of Aboriginal and European civilizations: images of Aboriginal boys in European clothing, an elder in chains, a defiant Aboriginal warrior, and a page from a 1940s document on methods of controlling the 'half-caste problem'. In the bottom right corner is a shopping list of colonial imports. *Crisis: what to do about this half-caste thing* encapsulates many of the themes running through urban art, and displays a brash confidence in dealing with the issues Aboriginal people face today.

185
186

184 Rick Roser, *Jundal gianga (woman powerful)*, 1990

185 Yvonne Koolmatrie,
Eel trap, 1990

186 (*below*) Richard Bell,
*Crisis: What to do about this
half-caste thing*, 1991

Not all the work of urban and rural artists is so politically and
socially charged. Their nineteenth-century forerunners, Tommy
McRae and others, provided commentaries on contemporary life and
portrayed traditional life for a non-Aboriginal public. Similarly
urban and rural artists today offer a variety of perspectives on a world
with which much of its audience has generally been unfamiliar. At the
same time, by implicitly questioning and challenging contemporary
attitudes, they articulate the concerns and aspirations of Aboriginal
people in modern society.

Conclusion

In 1988, when many Australians celebrated two centuries of European settlement, the Aboriginal community presented a varied response. Many Aboriginal people protested at the injustices of the past and the inequalities of the present; others saw the event as irrelevant, while some found cause to laud the benefits derived by Aboriginal society from European culture. Above all, Aboriginal people across the country celebrated the resilience of their culture in the face of great odds. A small group of artists in Ramingining in Central Arnhem Land, including Paddy Dhatangu, George Milpurrurru, Jimmy Wululu and David Malangi, decided to mark the event with a memorial to Aboriginal people past, present and future. The memorial took the form of two hundred hollow-log coffins or *dupun*, one to mark each year of settlement. The coffins, of the type used in reburial ceremonies throughout much of Arnhem Land, were painted with the clan designs and the major Dreamings of the artists. *The Aboriginal Memorial* project caught the imagination of artists in the local area until ultimately forty-three artists participated in its construction.

175, 187

The form of the *Memorial* fulfilled the intentions of the artists to commemorate the thousands of Aboriginal people who had perished in the course of European settlement, and for whom it had not been possible to conduct appropriate mortuary rites. The *Memorial's* relevance, however, is not confined to the past. It speaks of life, continuity, and a new beginning. An imposing forest of imagery, it confidently asserts a place for Aboriginal people in contemporary society. To fulfil its purposes, the artists intended the *Memorial* to be located in a public place where it could be preserved for future generations of Australians. One of the outstanding works of art to have been created in Australia, *The Aboriginal Memorial* is now permanently displayed in the National Gallery in Canberra.

The *Memorial* also symbolizes the significance of art to Aboriginal people today. On the one hand, it reflects traditional ceremonial and artistic activities which continue to be practised across the country, carrying the spiritual forces of the ancestral beings from one generation to the next. The recurring and inseparable themes of the land and the Dreaming are as pertinent now as they ever have been through countless past generations. The creative dramas of the ancestral beings continue to provide the template by which Aboriginal society relates to the natural and spiritual environment. On the other hand, the *Memorial* signifies the important role of art in expressing Aboriginal values and perspectives to a world which, in many cases, continues to be hostile to Aboriginal aspirations. The vital nature of Aboriginal culture is evident in the ways in which artists are taking the traditions of Aboriginal art, with conviction and integrity, to the world at large.

Aboriginal art, once admired solely for its antiquity, has now staked its claim on the artistic map of the modern world, as being among the great expressions of the human spirit and human experience.

187 Ramingining artists, *The Aboriginal Memorial*, 1988

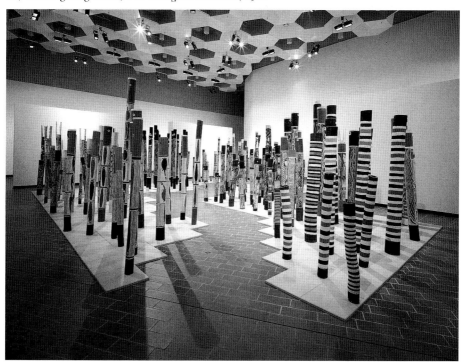

Acknowledgments

For their invaluable assistance in the preparation of this book, my gratitude goes to Kim Akerman, Michael Desmond, Djon Mundine and Daphne Wallace. Thanks also go to Banduk Marika, Margaret West, Luke Taylor, Diane Moon, Vivien Johnson, Christine Lennard, Steve Fox, Peter Sutton, Mrs P. Stanner, Peter Townsend, Joseph Caruana, and Betty Churcher and Kevin Munn and the staff of the National Gallery of Australia. The photography department of the Gallery deserves a special mention; it includes Gordon Reid, Bruce Moore, Willi Kemperman, Richard Pedvin and Robert Patterson. I would also like to thank all the institutions and collectors who provided the illustrations, and those individuals whose assistance has been most valuable. They include Christopher Anderson and Kate Alport, Kathy Barnes, Ace Bourke, Anne Marie Brody, Tim Burt and Josephine Gwynne, Helen Campbell, Julia Clark, Carol Cooper and Valerie Chapman, Judith Graham, Christopher Hodges, David Kaus and David Andre, Duncan Kentish, Mary Lakic, Mary Macha, Peter McKenzie, Michael O'Ferrall, Judith Ryan and Philip Jago, John E. Stanton and Ross Chadwick, Grahame L. Walsh, Margaret Waugh, and Daphne Williams and Janice Stanton. I would like to make special mention of James Mollison and of the late Anthony Forge. Finally, my deepest appreciation goes to the artists who have contributed to his volume, and to Aboriginal and Torres Strait Islander artists across the country, for sharing their art and their knowledge with us.

Note on Aboriginal names

The recording in writing of Aboriginal languages has only occurred since European colonization and there is no standardized orthography in use throughout Australia. Orthographies have changed over time, and vary not only from region to region, but often within a region and even within one language. Thus a Warlpiri-speaker living in or near Papunya, in the desert, might write his subsection name Tjakamarra, while a Warlpiri at Yuendumu would write Jakamarra, while yet a third may retain an earlier spelling, Jagamarra.

Most communities have adopted orthographic conventions, and where possible, these local conventions have been followed here.

Aboriginal languages contain many synonyms, including those of the names of creator ancestors, supernatural beings, cosmological phenomena, natural species and material objects. The use of many names is restricted to specific contextual situations, or to those people of relevant status. The Aboriginal words used in this volume are those used in a general public context.

Select Bibliography

Aboriginal Arts Board, *Oenpelli Bark Paintings*, Ure Smith, Sydney, 1979.

Akerman, K. with J.E. Stanton, *Jakuli: Kimberley pearlshell in Aboriginal Australia*, Museums and Art Galleries of the Northern Territory, Darwin, monograph series no. 4, in press.

Amadio, N. and R.G. Kimber, *Wildbird Dreaming: Aboriginal art from the Central Deserts of Australia*, Greenhouse Publications, Melbourne, 1987.

Bardon, G. *Aboriginal Art of the Western Desert*, Rigby, Adelaide, 1979.

—, *Papunya Tula: Art of the Western Desert*, McPhee Gribble, Melbourne, 1991.

Berndt, R.M. (ed.), *Australian Aboriginal Art*, Ure Smith, Sydney, 1964.

—, *The Australian Aboriginal heritage: An introduction through the arts*, Ure Smith, Sydney, 1974.

—, C.H. Berndt with J.E. Stanton, *Aboriginal Australian Art: A visual perspective*, Methuen Australia, Sydney, 1982.

Boulter, M., *The Art of Utopia; A new direction in contemporary Aboriginal art*, Craftsman House, Sydney, 1991.

Brandl, E.J., *Australian Aboriginal Paintings in Western and Central Arnhem Land*, Australian Institute of Aboriginal and Torres Strait Islander Studies, Canberra, 1973.

Brody, A.M., *Utopia: A Picture Story*, Heytesbury Holdings, Perth, Western Australia, 1990.

Caruana, W. (ed.), *Windows on the Dreaming: Aboriginal Paintings in the Australian National Gallery*, National Gallery of Australia, Canberra, and Ellsyd Press, Sydney, 1989.

Crawford, I.M., *The Art of the Wandjina: Aboriginal cave paintings in the Kimberley*, Western Australia, Oxford University Press, Melbourne, 1968.

Crocker, A. (ed.), *Mr. Sandman bring me a Dream*, Papunya Tula Artists, Alice Springs, and Aboriginal Artists Agency, Sydney, 1981.

Edwards, R. (ed.), *Aboriginal Art in Australia*, Ure Smith, Sydney, 1978.

—, and B. Guerin, *Aboriginal Bark Paintings*, Rigby, Adelaide, 1969.

Groger-Wurm, H.M., *Australian Aboriginal Bark Paintings and their Mythological Interpretation: Volume 1, Eastern Arnhem Land*, Australian Institute of Aboriginal and Torres Strait Islander Studies, Canberra, 1973.

Isaacs, J., *Australia's Living Heritage, Arts of the Dreaming*, Lansdowne Press, Sydney, 1984.

—, *Aboriginality: Contemporary Aboriginal paintings and prints*, University of Queensland Press, Brisbane, 1989.

Isaacs, J., *Desert Crafts: Anangu Maruku Punu*, Doubleday, Sydney, 1992.

Kupka, K., *Dawn of Art: Paintings and sculptures of Australian Aborigines*, Angus and Robertson, Sydney, 1965.

—, *Peintres Aborigenes d'Australie*, Musée de l'Homme, Paris, 1972.

Moore, D.R., *Arts and Crafts of Torres Strait*, Shire Ethnography, Aylesbury, UK, 1989.

Morphy, H. (ed.), *Animals into Art*, Unwin Hyman, London, 1989.

—, *Ancestral Connections*, The University of Chicago Press, Chicago and London, 1991.

Mountford, C.P., *Records of the American-Australian Scientific Expedition to Arnhem Land, Volume 1; Art, Myth and Symbolism*, Melbourne University Press, Melbourne, 1956.

—, *The Tiwi: Their Art, Myth and Ceremony*, Phoenix House, London, 1958.

Mundine, D., *Gamununggu: Bark Paintings*, Art Gallery of New South Wales, Sydney, in press.

Munn, N.D., *Walbiri Iconography*, The University of Chicago Press, Chicago and London, 1986 (1973).

O'Ferrall, M.A., *Keepers of the Secrets: Aboriginal Art from Arnhem Land*, Art Gallery of Western Australia, Perth, 1990.

Spencer, W.B., *Native Tribes of the Northern Territory of Australia*, Macmillan, London, 1914.

Stanton, J.E., *Painting the Country: Contemporary Aboriginal art from the Kimberley region*, Western Australia, The University of Western Australia Press, Perth, Western Australia, 1989.

Sutton, P. (ed.), *Dreamings: The Art of Aboriginal Australia*, Viking Press, New York, 1988.

Ucko, P.J., (ed.), *Form in Indigenous Art*, Australian Institute of Aboriginal and Torres Strait Islander Studies, Canberra, 1977.

Walsh, G.L., *Australia's Greatest Rock Art*, E.J. Brill/Robert Brown, Bathurst, New South Wales, 1988.

Exhibition catalogues

Barou, J.P. and S. Crossman (eds.), *L'été australien à Montpellier: 100 chefs-d'œuvre de la peinture australienne*, Libération, Paris, and Musée Fabre, Montpellier, 1990.

Berndt, R.M., and C.H. Berndt, *An Exhibition of Aboriginal Art: Arnhem Land paintings on bark and carved human figures*, Western Australian Museum, Perth, 1957.

Brody, A.M., *The Face of the Centre: Papunya Tula paintings, 1971–84*, National Gallery of Victoria, Melbourne, 1985.

—, *Contemporary Aboriginal Art: The Robert Holmes à Court Collection*, Heytesbury Holdings, Perth, Western Australia, 1990.

Cooper, C. et al, *Aboriginal Australia*, Australian Gallery Directors Council Ltd, Sydney, 1981.

Eather, M. and M. Hall, *Balance: Views, Visions, Influences*, Queensland Art Gallery, Brisbane, 1990.

Gunn, G., *Groote Eylandt art: Leonhard Adam Ethnological Collection, part one*, University of Melbourne, Melbourne, 1973.

Johnson, T. and V. Johnson, *Koori Art '84*, Artspace, Sydney, 1984.

Johnson, V., *Art & Aboriginality 1987*, Aspex Gallery, Portsmouth, UK, 1987.

—, et al, *The Painted Dream: Contemporary Aboriginal Paintings from the Tim and Vivien Johnson Collection*, Auckland City Art Gallery, Auckland, New Zealand, 1990.

Jones, P.G. and P.J. Sutton, *Art and Land, Aboriginal Sculptures of the Lake Eyre Region*, South Australian Museum, Adelaide, 1986.

Luthi, B. (ed.), *Aratjara: Australian Aboriginal Art*, Kunstammlung Nordrhein-Westfalen, Düsseldorf, 1993.

Maughan, J. and J. Zimmer (eds.), *Dot and Circle: a retrospective survey of the Aboriginal acrylic paintings of Central Australia*, Royal Melbourne Institute of Technology, Melbourne, 1986.

Mundine, D. with F. Foley, *Tyerabarrbowaryaou: I shall never become a white man*, Museum of Contemporary Art, Sydney, 1992.

O'Ferrall, M.A., *On the Edge; Five Contemporary Aboriginal Artists*, Art Gallery of Western Australia, Perth, 1989.

—, *1990 Venice Biennale. Australia: Rover Thomas – Trevor Nickolls*, Art Gallery of Western Australia, Perth, 1990.

Perkins, H., *Aboriginal Women's Exhibition*, Art Gallery of New South Wales, Sydney, 1991.

Ryan, J., *Mythscapes: Aboriginal Art of the Desert*, National Gallery of Victoria, Melbourne, 1989.

—, *Spirit in Land: Bark Paintings from Arnhem Land*, National Gallery of Victoria, Melbourne, 1990.

—, (ed.), *Images of Power: Aboriginal Art of the Kimberley*, National Gallery of Victoria, Melbourne, 1993.

Wallace, D., M. Desmond and W. Caruana, *Flash Pictures by Aboriginal and Torres Strait Islander Artists*. National Gallery of Australia, Canberra, 1991.

West, M.K.C. (ed.), *The Inspired Dream*, Queensland Art Gallery, Brisbane, 1988.

List of Illustrations

The artist's language group and dates of birth and death follow the name. Avoidance of the spoken names of the recently deceased is customary in Aboriginal communities, and this custom should be respected. In some cases the biographical details are approximate, as indicated, or unknown due to the lack of records. Dimensions of works are given in centimetres and inches, height preceding width.

Abbreviations for the collections are:

AGNSW Art Gallery of New South Wales, Sydney
AGSA Art Gallery of South Australia, Adelaide
AGWA Art Gallery of Western Australia, Perth
AIATSIS Australian Institute of Aboriginal and Torres Strait Islander Studies Pictorial Collection, Canberra
AM The Australian Museum, Sydney
MAGNT Museums and Art Galleries of the Northern Territory, Darwin
MOV Museum of Victoria, Melbourne. Reproduced with the permission of the Museum Council
NGA National Gallery of Australia, Canberra
NGA/AC National Gallery of Australia, Canberra. Purchased from Gallery admission charges
NGV National Gallery of Victoria, Melbourne
NMA National Museum of Australia, Canberra
RHàC The Robert Holmes à Court Collection
SAM South Australian Museum, Adelaide
WU University of Western Australia, Berndt Museum of Anthropology, Perth
AAA Copyright: Aboriginal Artists Agency, Sydney

1 Jack Wunuwun (Djinang, 1930–90). *Banumbirr the Morning Star*, 1987. Natural pigments on bark 178 × 125 (70⅛ × 49¼). NGA/AC.
2 Rock painting, Ubirr, Kakadu, Northern Territory. Photo Reg Morrison/Auscape.
3 Map drawn by Annick Petersen.
4 Rock engraving, *c*. AD 500, Mount Cameron West, Tasmania. Photo Robert Edwards.
5 Rock painting of lightning figures, Katherine River, Northern Territory. Photo Grahame L. Walsh.
6 Hand stencil, 9–20,000 before present, Kakadu, Northern Territory. Photo Grahame L. Walsh.
7 Narrative rock painting, Musgrave Ranges, South Australia. Photo Grahame L. Walsh.
8 Bradshaw figures, Kimberley, Western Australia. Photo Grahame L. Walsh.
9 Rock drawing of kangaroos, Wilton, New

South Wales. Photo Grahame L. Walsh.
10 George French Angus. *Native weapons and implements*, 1847. *South Australian Illustrated*, London 1847. NGA.
11 Najombolmi (Kunwinjku, *c*.1895–1967). *Hunter*, 1960s. Rock painting, extended figure h. 142 (56). Djerlandjal site, Kakadu, Northern Territory. Photo Grahame L. Walsh.
12 Unknown artist. Gunbalanya, West Arnhem Land. *Mimi spearing a kangaroo*, 1912. Natural pigments on bark 127.5 × 80 (50¼ × 31½). MOV. Baldwin Spencer Collection.
13 Jimmy Midjaw Midjaw (Kunwinjku, 1897–*c*.1985) *Nadulmi in his kangaroo manifestation, as Wubarr leader*, 1950. Natural pigments on bark 76 × 58 (29⅞ × 22⅞). WU.
14 Paddy Compass Namatbara (Iwaidja, 1890–1973). *Maam spirit*, *c*.1963. Natural pigments on bark 58 × 35 (22⅞ × 13¾). NGA. Founding Donor Fund.
15 Bobby Barrdjaray Nganjmira (Kunwinjku, 1915–92), *Kangaroo and crocodile*, 1984. Natural pigments on bark 151 × 88 (59½ × 34⅝). NGA.
16 Bruce Nabckeyo (Kunwinjku, b. *c*.1949). *Yingarna, the Rainbow Serpent*, 1989. Natural pigments on bark 150.1 × 40.4 (59⅛ × 15⅞). NGA.
17 Robin Nganjmira (Kunwinjku, 1951–91). *Likanaya*, 1989. Natural pigments on bark 191 × 81 (75¼ × 31⅞). NGA.
18 Djawida (Kunwinjku, b. 1936). *Nawura, Dreamtime ancestor spirit*, 1985. Natural pigments on bark 156 × 68 (61⅜ × 26⅞). NGA.
19 Peter Marralwanga (Kuninjku, 1916–87). *Ngalyod, the Rainbow Serpent*, 1981. Natural pigments on bark 154 × 93 (60⅝ × 36⅝). NGA.
20 Crusoe Kuningbal (Kuninjku, 1922–84). *Mimi spirits*. 1979. Natural pigments on wood h. 216 (85) and 221 (87). NGA.
21 John Mawandjul (Kuninjku, b. 1952). *Rainbow Serpent's antilopine kangaroo*, 1991. Natural pigments on bark 189 × 94 (74⅜ × 37). NGA.
22 Mick Kubaku (Kuninjku, b. 1925), *Dird*, 1991. Natural pigments on bark 196.5 × 74 (77⅜ × 29⅛). NGA.
23 Wally Mandarrk (Dangbon, 1915–87). *Narrangem and Naldaluk, Lightning Spirits*, 1986. Natural pigments on bark 89.5 × 27 (35¼ × 10⅝). NGA/AC.
24 Ronnie Djambardi (Kurrkoni, b. 1925). *Wandurk and his two wives*, 1981. Natural

pigments on bark 140 × 45 (55¼ × 17¾).
25 Les Midikuria (Rembarrnga, b. *c*.1943). *Digging sticks and sacred dilly bag at Ginajangga*, 1988. Natural pigments on bark 152 × 93.8 (59⅞ × 36⅞). AGSA. Maude Vizard-Wholohan Art Prize Purchase Award 1988.
26 England Bangala (Gunardba, b. *c*.1925). *Modj (Rainbow Serpent)*, 1988. Natural pigments on bark 143.5 × 83 (56½ × 32⅔). NGA.
27 Dorothy Galalebda (Gunardba, b. *c*.1967). *Djinggabardabiya (triangular pandanus skirt)*, 1989. Natural pigments on bark 168 × 92 (66⅛ × 36¼). NGA.
28 Lena Yaringura (Rembarrnga, b. 1948). *Bok'narru, Rembarrnga male dancing belt*, 1989. Fibres, natural pigments, wax, feathers, length 83 (32⅝). NGA.
29 Lena Djamaraku (Rembarrnga, b. 1943). *Djerrh, bush string carrying bag*, 1989. Fibres, natural dyes, feathers w. 49 (19¼). NGA.
30 Jack Kala Kala (Rembarrnga, *c*.1925–87). *Balangu, two sharks*, 1986. Natural pigments on bark 130 × 60 (51⅛ × 23⅝). NGA.
31 Paddy Fordham Wainburranga (Rembarrnga, b. 1938). *How World War II began (through the eyes of the Rembarrnga)*, 1990. Natural pigments on bark 65 × 135 (25⅝ × 53⅛). NGA.
32 Brian Nyinawanga (Rembarrnga, b. 1935). *Bones*, 1980. Natural pigments, wood, paperbark, cotton, string, size variable. MAGNT.
33 Tjam (Sam) Yilkarri Kitani (Liyagalawumirri, 1891–1956). *Wagilag*, 1937. Natural pigments on bark 126.5 × 68.5 (49¾ × 27). MOV. Donald Thomson Collection.
34 Dawidi Djulwarak (Liyagalawumirri, 1921–70). *Wagilag religious story*, 1965. Natural pigments on bark 84 × 46.5 (33⅛ × 18¼). Private Collection.
35 Paddy Dhatangu (Liyagalawumirri, b. 1915). *The Wagilag Sisters story*, 1983. Natural pigments on bark; 60 × 133 (23⅝ × 52⅜). NGA/AC.
36 Peter Bandjuljul (Djinang, b. 1942). *Djang'kawu creator ancestors and Gachalan the goanna at Mewirnbi*, 1982. Natural pigments on bark 127.5 × 90 (50¼ × 35⅜). NGA/AC.
37 Tom Djawa (Gupapuyngu, 1905–80). *Crabs*, 1969. Natural pigments on bark 101.5 × 50 (40 × 19⅝). NGA.
38 David Malangi (Manharrngu, b. 1927). *Gunmirringgu*, 1967. Natural pigments on

210

bark 124.5 × 69 (49 × 27¼). MAGNT. Groger-Wurm Collection.

39 Don Gundinga (Djinang, 1941–89). *Honey Dreaming at Walkumbimirri*, 1984. Natural pigments on bark 142.5 × 83 (56⅛ × 32⅝). NGA. Founding Donor Fund.

40 Jimmy Wululu (Daygurrgurr/Gupapuyngu, b. 1936). *Niwuda, Yirritja native honey*, 1986. Natural pigments on bark 144 × 60 (56¾ × 23⅝). NGA.

41 George Milpurrurru (Ganalbingu, b. 1934). *Fire and Water Dreaming*, 1989. Natural pigments on bark 200.5 × 76 (78⅞ × 29⅞). NGA.

42 Clara Wubugwubuk (Ganalbingu, b. 1950). *Walmi grass – munyigani edible tuber*, 1990. Natural pigments on bark 211 × 67 (83⅛ × 26⅜). John W. Kluge Collection.

43 Johnny Bulun Bulun (Ganalbingu, b. 1946). *Sacred waterholes surrounded by totemic animals of the artist's clan*, 1981. Natural pigments on bark 135.5 × 73 (53⅜ × 28¾). NGA.

44 Wandjuk Marika (Rirratjingu, 1927–87). *The birth of the Djang'kawu children at Yalangbara*, 1982. Natural pigments on bark 147.5 × 66 (58 × 26). NGA/AC. (AAA).

45 Mick Daypurryun (Liyagawumirri, b. 1929). *Sacred waterholes – the Djang'kawu*, 1988. Natural pigments on bark 173.7 × 67.3 (68⅜ × 26½). AGWA.

46 Mandjuwi (Galpu, b. 1934) with Kallie Yalkarrawuy (Galpu, b. 1942). *The Morning Star ceremony*, 1979 (installation). Natural pigments on bark and wood, feathers, fibres, string h. 209 (82¼). NGA.

47 Mawalan Marika (Rirratjingu, 1908–67). *Turtle Dreaming*, c.1963. Natural pigments on bark 132 × 35 (52 × 13¾). NGA.

48 Banduk Marika (Rirratjingu, b. 1954). *Minyapa ga Dhanggatjiya*, 1990. Linocut on paper 61 × 117 (24 × 46⅛). NGA. Gordon Darling Fund 1991. (AAA).

49 Mathaman Marika (Rirratjingu, c.1920–70). *Wagilak ceremony*, 1963. Natural pigments on bark 157.5 × 62.8 (62 × 24¾). NGV. Donated by Mr James A. Davidson 1967.

50 Dundiwuy Wanambi (Marrakulu, b. 1936). *Wuyal creation story with Gundimulk ceremonial ground*, 1990. Natural pigments on bark 183 × 64.5 (72 × 25⅜). NGV.

51 Badangga (Wangurri, 1910–c.1970) and Waninyambi (Warramiri, b. 1902?) *Djirrban*, 1960. Natural pigments on wood, fibres h. 178 (70⅛). WU.

52 Birrikidji Gumana (Dhalwangu, c.1898–1982). *Lany'tjung story – the death of Lany'tjung*, 1960s. Natural pigments on bark 135.8 × 63.8 (53⅜ × 25⅛). AGWA.

53 Yanggarriny Wunungmurra (Dhalwangu, b. 1932), *Minhala the Long-Necked Tortoise on the sacred log*, 1990. Natural pigments on wood, h. 132.5 (52⅛). NGA.

54 Munggarrawuy Yunupingu (Gumatj, c.1907–79). *Lany'tjung story number two*, 1959. Natural pigments on bark 193 × 73.7 (76 × 29). AGNSW. Gift of Dr Stuart Scougall 1959.

55 Mutitjpuy Munungpurr (Djapu, b. 1932). *Dugong hunt*, 1967. Natural pigments on bark 118 × 54 (46½ × 21¼). NMA. Groger-Wurm Collection.

56 Wakuthi Marawili (Madarrpa, b. 1921). *Fire Dreaming with Dugong hunting story*, 1982. Natural pigments on bark 139 × 47 (54¾ × 18½). NGA/AC.

57 Liwukang Bukurlatjpi (Warramiri, b. c.1927). *Mamu spirit boat*, 1982. Natural pigments on bark 124.5 × 38 (49 × 15). NGA/AC.

58 Narritjin Maymuru (Manggalili, 1922–80). *Nyapililngu at Djarrakpi*, c.1978. Natural pigments on bark 158 × 60 (62¼ × 23⅝). NGA/AC.

59 Luma Luma Yunupingu (Gumatj, 1941–85). *The spirit's journey*, 1984. Natural pigments on bark and wood, painting 198 × 80 (78 × 31½), sculptures h. 139 (54⅝) and 147 (57⅞). NGA. Founding Donor Fund.

60 George Jawaranga Wurramara (Anindilyakwa, 1926–88). *Yinikarrka (the Wind Spirit)*, 1984. Natural pigments on bark 96 × 40 (37¾ × 15¾). NGA. Founding Donor Fund.

61 Ginger Riley Munduwalawala (Mara, b. 1937). *My country*, 1988. Synthetic polymer on canvas 178 × 247 (70⅛ × 97¼). Anthony and Beverley Waldegrave-Knight Collection.

62 Bill Namiayangwa (Anindilyakwa, 1923–68). *They surround a man and his five wives, but he escapes*, c.1955 (detail from the series *An attack by war canoes*). Natural pigments on bark 24 × 38 (9½ × 15). NGA.

63 Minimini Mamarika (Anindilyakwa, 1904–72). *Orion and the Pleiades*, 1948. Natural pigments on bark 76 × 32 (29⅞ × 12⅝). AGSA. Gift of the Commonwealth Government 1957.

64 Attributed to Nandabitta (Anindilyakwa, 1911–81). *Macassan prahu and trepang curing*, c.1974. Natural pigments on bark 62 × 41 (24⅜ × 16⅛). NGA/AC.

65 Marruwani (Tiwi, 1916-deceased). *The death of Purukuparli*, 1954. Natural pigments on bark 89 × 24 (35 × 9½). SAM.

66 Wilfred Nalandarra (Ritangu, b. 1917). *Fish and birds in the shallows*, 1989. Synthetic polymer on canvas 170 × 181 (66⅞ × 71⅛). Private Collection.

67 Willie Gudipi (Alawa, b. 1916). *Untitled*, 1990. Synthetic polymer on canvas 173 × 110.9 (68⅛ × 43⅝). NGA.

68 Amy Johnson Jirwulurr (Wagilak, b. 1953). *Some animals have secret songs*, 1990. Synthetic polymer on canvas 175 × 167 (68⅞ × 65¾). Anthony and Beverley Waldegrave-Knight Collection.

69 Laurie Nelson Tuki-al-ila (b. c.1923), Bob One Gala-ding-wama (b. 1925), Big Jack Yarunga (b. 1905), Don Burak-madjua (b. 1925), Charlie Quiet Kwangdini (b. 1905) and one unknown artist (Tiwi). *Pukumani poles*, 1958 (a group of 17 graveposts from Milikapati, Melville Island). Natural pigments on ironwood, h. 147.3–274.2 (58–108). AGNSW. Gift of Dr Stuart Scougall 1958.

70 Bama Yu (Polly Miller) (Tiwi, 1921–89). *Jimwalini, Pukumani basket*, 1984. Natural pigments on bark, fibre h. 65 (25⅝). NGA/AC.

71 Unknown artist (Tiwi). Bathurst Island, Northern Territory. *Pamijini mourning band*, pre-1912. Natural pigments, abrus seeds, feathers, cane h. 83 (32⅝). MOV. Baldwin Spencer Collection.

72 Mani Luki (Harry Carpenter) (Tiwi, c.1905-deceased). *Bima carrying Jinani*, c.1970, (detail from the installation *The Purukuparli and Bima story*, by Mani Luki, Paddy Henry Ripijingimpi and other artists). Natural pigments on ironwood, fibres, max. h. 180 (70⅞). MAGNT. The Holmes Tiwi Collection.

73 Enraeld Djulabiyanna (Tiwi, 1895–c.1965). *Purukuparli and Bima*, c.1955. Natural pigments on ironwood h. 60 (23⅝) and 53 (20⅞). NGA/AC.

74 Paddy Henry Ripijingimpi (Tiwi, b. 1925). *Bird*, 1979. Natural pigments on ironwood 103 × 16 × 20.5 (40½ × 6¼ × 8⅛). NGA.

75 Nellie Wanterapila (Tiwi, 1905–79). *Coral*, 1974. Natural pigments on bark 37.5 × 62 (14¾ × 24⅜). NGA.

76 Declan Apuatimi (Tiwi, 1930–85). *Clubs*, c.1984. Natural pigments on canvas 90 × 90 (35⅜ × 35⅝). NGA.

77 Bede Tungutalum (Tiwi, b. 1952), Tiwi Designs (established 1969). *Yam design*, 1982. Screenprint on cotton; detail. Tiwi Designs.

78 Thecla Puruntatameri (Tiwi, b. 1971). *Irramari*, 1991. Gouache on paper 56.3 × 76 (22⅛ × 29⅞). NGA.

79 Charles Mardigan (Murrinh-Garr, 1926–86). *Billabongs*, 1961. Natural pigments on bark 63.2 × 37.8 (24⅞ × 14⅞). AGNSW. Gift of Dr Stuart Scougall 1961.

80 Simon Ngumbe (Murrinh-Patha, b. 1911). *Rainbow Snake and children*, c.1972. Natural pigments on bark 62 × 24.6 (24⅜ × 9⅝). AGWA.

81 Robin Nilco (Murrinh-Amor, b. 1956). *Water python and boomerangs*, 1990. Synthetic polymer on canvas 45 × 152.5 (17¾ × 60). NGA.

82 Nym Bunduk (Murrinh-Patha, c.1907–81). *Map of the Murrinh-Patha countryside*, 1959. Natural pigments on composition board 89 × 156 (35 × 61⅜). Private Collection.

83 Paddy Jupurrurla Nelson (b. 1920), Paddy Japaljarri Sims (b. 1917), Paddy Cookie Japaljarri Stewart (b. 1940), Neville Japangardi Poulson (b. c.1950), Francis Jupurrurla Kelly (b. c. 1950) and Frank Bronson Jakamarra Nelson (b. 1948) (Warlpiri). *Yarla*, 1989 (ground painting in the exhibition *Magiciens de la terre*, organized by the Centre Georges Pompidou). Earth pigments, mixed media 4 × 10 m. (13 × 33 ft). Photo Centre Georges Pompidou, Paris.

84 Various artists (Diyari). Killalpaninna, South Australia. *A group of toas*, 1904–05. Natural pigments on wood, max. h. 57 (22½). SAM.

85 Unknown artist (Pitjantjatjara). Amata, South Australia. *Animal carving*, 1977. Wood, length 114 (44⅞). SAM.

86 Angkuna Graham (Pitjantjatjara, b. 1943), Ernabella Arts (established 1949). *Untitled*, 1984. Batik on silk 93 × 376 (36⅝ × 148). NGA. Founding Donor Fund.

87 Kay Tunkun (Pitjantjatjara, b. 1957). *Kipara (Wild Turkey) Dreaming*, 1986–87. Watercolour on paper 47 × 80 (18½ × 31½). Private Collection.

88 Sadie Singer (Pitjantjatjara, b. 1950). *Summer landscape*, 1988. Lithograph on paper 66.8 × 52.4 (26¼ × 20⅝). NGA. Gordon Darling Fund 1989.

89 Albert Namatjira (Arrernte, 1902–59). *Anthewerre*, *c*.1955. Watercolour on paper 24.5 × 35.2 (9⅝ × 13¾). NGA. Gift of Thomas William and Pamela Joyce (Joy) Falconer, Canberra. Reproduced by permission of Legend Press Pty. Ltd., Sydney, Australia.

90 Billy Stockman Tjapaltjarri (Anmatyerre/Arrernte, b. *c*.1927), Long Jack Phillipus Tjakamarra (Warlpiri/Luritja, b. *c*.1932), Kaapa Tjampitjinpa (Anmatyerre/Arrernte, 1920–89), Old Mick Tjakamarra (Luritja/Warlpiri, b. *c*.1914) and other artists. *Honey Ant Dreaming*, 1971 (mural at Papunya School). Photo H. Munro, Geoffrey Bardon Collection.

91 Long Jack Phillipus Tjakamarra (Warlpiri/Luritja, b. *c*.1932). *Children's Kadaitcha Dreaming*, 1972. Synthetic polymer on board 56 × 35 (22 × 13¼). Private Collection. (AAA).

92 Charlie Tjaruru Tjungurrayi (Pintupi, b. 1921). *Mitukatjirri*, 1972. Gouache on composition board 32.8 × 65.1 (12⅞ × 25⅝). NGV. Presented by Mrs Douglas Carnegie OAM, 1988. (AAA).

93 Dinny Nolan Tjampitjinpa (Warlpiri, b. *c*.1924). *Shield*, 1972. Natural pigments on wood h. 74.5 (29⅜). NMA. (AAA).

94 Johnny Warrangula Tjupurrula (Luritja, b. 1918). *Nintaka and the Mala (Wallaby) Men*, 1973. Synthetic polymer on composition board 69.6 × 65.2 (27⅜ × 25⅝). NGV. Purchased through the Art Foundation of Victoria with funds provided by ICI Australia Ltd., Fellow, 1988. (AAA).

95 Ronnie Tjampitjinpa (Pintupi, b. *c*.1943). *Two Women Dreaming*, 1990. Synthetic polymer on canvas 150.2 × 182.4 (59⅛ × 71⅞). NGA. (AAA).

96 Turkey Tolson Tjupurrula (Pintupi, b. 1938). *Straightening spears at Ilyingaungau*, 1990. Synthetic polymer on canvas 181.5 × 243.5 (71½ × 95⅞). AGSA. Gift of the Friends of the AGSA 1990. (AAA).

97 Anatjari Tjampitjinpa (Pintupi, b. 1927). *Ceremonial ground at Kulkuta*, 1981. Synthetic polymer on canvas 182.5 × 182 (71⅞ × 71⅝). Tim and Vivien Johnson Collection. (AAA).

98 Mick Namarari Tjapaltjarri (Pintupi, b. 1926). *Bandicoot Dreaming*, 1991. Synthetic polymer on canvas 182 × 150 (71⅝ × 59). MAGNT. (AAA).

99 Uta Uta Tjangala (Pintupi, 1920–90). *The Old Man's Dreaming*, 1983. Synthetic polymer on canvas 242 × 362 (95¼ × 142½). AGSA. South Australian Government Grant 1985. (AAA).

100 Tim Leura Tjapaltjarri (Anmatyerre/Arrernte, *c*. 1936–84). *Men's camps at Lyrrpurrung Ngturra*, 1979. Synthetic polymer on canvas 218 × 260 (85⅞ × 102⅜). NGA/AC. (AAA).

101 Clifford Possum Tjapaltjarri (Anmatyerre/Arrernte, b. *c*.1943). *Honey Ant Dreaming story*, 1983. Synthetic polymer on canvas 244 × 366 (96⅛ × 144⅛). NGV. (AAA).

102 Tim Leura Tjapaltjarri (Anmatyerre/Arrernte, *c*.1936–84) with Clifford Possum Tjapaltjarri (Anmatyerre/Arrernte, b. *c*.1943). *Napperby Death Spirit Dreaming*, 1980. Synthetic polymer on canvas 213 × 701

(83⅞ × 276). NGV. Felton Bequest 1988. (AAA).

103 Michael Jagamarra Nelson (Warlpiri, b. 1949). *Five Dreamings*, 1984. Synthetic polymer on canvas 122 × 182 (48 × 71⅝). Gabrielle Pizzi Collection. (AAA).

104 Sonder Nampitjinpa (Warlpiri, b. 1956). *Pankalangu ceremonies at Yamunturnga*, 1987. Coolamon: synthetic polymer on wood, length 131.2 (51⅝). NGA/AC. (AAA).

105 Pansy Napangati (Luritja/Warlpiri, b. *c*.1947). *Old Man at Ilpilli*, 1990. Synthetic polymer on canvas 90 × 137 (35⅜ × 53⅞). Private Collection. (AAA).

106 Maxie Tjampitjinpa (Warlpiri, b. *c*.1945). *Flying Ant Dreaming at Wantungurru*, 1988. Synthetic polymer on canvas 233 × 213 (91¾ × 83⅞). NGA. (AAA).

107 Paddy Japaljarri Sims (Warlpiri, b. 1917). *Ngapakurlu (Rain)*, 1983. Synthetic polymer on Yuendumu School door. Photo Gerry Orkin. AIATSIS.

108 Darby Jampijinpa Ross (Warlpiri, b. *c*.1910). *Emu Dreaming*, 1987. Synthetic polymer on canvas 121.1 × 91.5 (47⅝ × 36). NGV. Purchased from funds donated by Lauraine Diggins 1988.

109 Paddy Jupurrurla Nelson (b. 1920), Paddy Japaljarri Sims (b. 1917) and Larry Jungarrayi Spencer (1919–90) (Warlpiri). *Yanjilypiri Jukurrpa (Star Dreaming)*, 1985. Synthetic polymer on canvas 372 × 171.4 (146½ × 67½). NGA/AC.

110 Liddy Napanangka Walker (b. 1930), Topsy Napanangka (b. 1924) and Judy Nampijinpa Granites (b. 1934) (Warlpiri). *Wakirlpirri Jukurrpa*, 1985. Synthetic polymer on canvas 124.6 × 123.8 (49 × 48¾). NGA/AC.

111 Uni Nampijinpa Martin (b. *c*.1942) and Dolly Nampijinpa Daniels (formerly Granites, b. 1931) (Warlpiri). *Warlukurlangu (Fire Country) Dreaming*, 1988. Synthetic polymer on canvas 182.4 × 121.8 (71¾ × 48). NGV.

112 Peggy Napurrurla Poulson (b. *c*.1935), Maggie Napurrurla Poulson (b. *c*.1935) and Bessie Nakamarra Sims (b. *c*.1940) (Warlpiri). *Janganpa Jukurrpa (Possum Dreaming)*, 1988. Synthetic polymer on canvas 210 × 91 (82⅝ × 35⅞). Tim and Vivien Johnson Collection.

113 Jeannie Nungarrayi Egan (Warlpiri, b. 1948). *Jardiwampa Jukurrpa (Snake Dreaming)*, 1989. Synthetic polymer on canvas 122 × 183 (48 × 72). NGV.

114 Clarise Nampijinpa Poulson (Warlpiri, b. *c*.1954). *Pamapardu Jukurrpa (Flying Ant Dreaming)*, 1990. Synthetic polymer on canvas 183 × 91 (72 × 35⅞). Collection of Dr Kingsley Gee.

115 Molly Napurrurla Tasman (Warlpiri, b. *c*.1955). *Marsupial Mouse Dreaming at Marlungurru*, 1986. Mixed media on cardboard 83.8 × 58.8 (33 × 23⅛). NGV. Purchased through The Art Foundation of Victoria from funds provided by CRA Limited, Fellow, 1989.

116 Peter Blacksmith Japanangka (Kartangarurru, *c*.1918–91). *Snake Dreaming*, 1986. Synthetic polymer and house paint on canvas 210.4 × 110.5 (82⅞ × 43½). NGV. Purchased through The Art Foundation of Victoria

from funds provided by CRA Limited, Fellow, 1989.

117 Abie Jangala (Warlpiri, b. 1919). *Water Dreaming*, 1987. Synthetic polymer on canvas 122 × 92 (48 × 36¼). RHàC.

118 Jimmy Jampijinpa Robertson (Warlpiri, b. 1946). *Seed Dreaming*, 1986. Synthetic polymer on canvas 217.9 × 120.6 (85¾ × 47½). NGV. Purchased through The Art Foundation of Victoria from funds provided by CRA Limited, Fellow, 1989.

119 Edie Kemarre (Alyawarre, b. *c*.1950), Utopia Women's Batik Group (established 1978). *Women sitting in groups painting each other for corroboree*, 1987. Batik on silk 113 × 386 (44½ × 152). NGA.

120 Sandra Holmes Kemarre (Alyawarre, b. *c*.1955), Utopia Women's Batik Group (established 1978). *Morning Star Dreaming*, 1988. Batik on silk, approx. 120 × 240 (47¼ × 94½). RHàC.

121 Mavis Holmes Petyarre (Anmatyerre, b. *c*.1947). *Untitled*, 1989. Synthetic polymer on car door h. 99 (39). NGA.

122 Lindsay Bird Mpetyane (Anmatyerre, b. *c*.1935). *Utnea*, 1991. Synthetic polymer on canvas 150 × 250 (59 × 98⅜). Utopia Art Sydney.

123 Emily Kame Kngwarreye (Anmatyerre, b. *c*.1916). *Untitled*, 1991. Synthetic polymer on canvas 250 × 150 (98⅜ × 59). NGA.

124 Lilly Sandover Kngwarreye (Alyawarre, b. *c*.1937). *Sandover River*, 1989. Synthetic polymer on canvas 126 × 125 (49⅝ × 49¼). RHàC.

125 Ada Bird Petyarre (Anmatyerre, b. *c*.1930). *Sacred grasses*, 1989. Synthetic polymer on canvas 130 × 230 (51⅛ × 90½). NGV.

126 Peter Sunfly (Sandfly) Tjampitjin (Kukatja, b. *c*.1916). *Sleeping at Naligudjana*, 1986. Synthetic polymer on canvasboard 50 × 60 (19⅝ × 23⅝). AGWA.

127 Donkeyman Lee Tjupurrula (Kukatja, b. 1921). *Untitled*, 1989. Synthetic polymer on canvas 120 × 180 (47¼ × 70⅞). NGV.

128 Susie Bootja Bootja Napangarti (Kukatja, b. *c*.1932). *Kutal soakage*, 1989. Synthetic polymer on canvas 159.5 × 80 (62⅞ × 31½). RHàC.

129 Wimminji Tjapangarti (Kukatja, b. *c*.1925). *The artist's country*, 1989. Synthetic polymer on canvas 90 × 120 (35⅜ × 47¼). NGA.

130 Patricia Lee Napangarti (Warlpiri, b. 1960). *The death of the Tjampitjin fighting man at Tjunta*, 1989. Synthetic polymer on canvas 180 × 120 (70⅞ × 47¼). NGA.

131 Jimmy Pike (Walmajarri, b. 1940). *Jamirtilangu Parrija Purrku II*, 1987. Synthetic polymer on canvas 60.7 × 50.6 (23⅞ × 19⅞). RHàC.

132 Rhonda Lightning (Jaru/Walmajarri, b. *c*.1920). *The Dingo and the Emu*, 1983. Natural pigments and ink on canvasboard 51 × 61 (20⅛ × 24). WU.

133 Jarinyanu David Downs (Wangkajunga/Walmajarri, b. *c*.1925). *Moses and Aaron leading the Jewish people across the Red Sea*, 1989. Synthetic polymer and ochre on canvas 198 × 137 (78 × 53⅞). NGA.

134 Peter Skipper (Juwaliny/Walmajarri, b. *c*.1929). *Kurrkuminti Kurrkuminti*, 1987. Synthetic polymer on canvas 198 × 122 (78 × 48). RHàC.

135 Wandjina figures, Mandanggari, Gibb River, Kimberley, Western Australia. Photo Howard McNickle. AIATSIS.

136 Charlie Numbulmoore (Ngarinyin, c. 1907–c.1971). *Wandjina-kaluru beings at Mamadai*, 1970. Natural pigments on bark 110 × 71 (43¼ × 28). NMA.

137 Alex Mingelmanganu (Kulari/Wunambal, died 1981). *Wandjina*, 1980. Natural pigments and oil on canvas 159 × 139.5 (62⅝ × 54¾). NGA.

138 Unknown artist (Karajarri). Kimberley, Western Australia. Pearlshell, charcoal h. 17 (6¾). NMA. Elkin Collection.

139 Unknown artist (Bardi or Nyul Nyul). Lombadina, Western Australia. *Pendant; Minnimb the whale*, 1988. Pearlshell, ochre, hairstring; pearlshell h. 17.5 (6⅞). NGA/AC.

140 John Dodo (Karajarri, b. 1910). *Kungolo*, 1987. Natural pigments on stone 28 × 13 × 17.5 (11 × 5⅛ × 6⅞). NGA.

141 Paddy Jaminji (Kija, b. 1912). *Manginta the Devil Devil*, c.1977 (from the *Kuril Kuril* ceremonial series). Natural pigments on board 119 × 71.9 (46⅞ × 28⅜). NMA.

142 Rover Thomas (Kukatja/Wangkajunga, b. 1926). *Cyclone Tracy*, 1991. Natural pigments on canvas 183 × 168 (72 × 66⅛). NGA.

143 Jock Mosquito Jubarljari (Jaru, b. 1951). *Kawarrin*, 1984. Natural pigments on board 90 × 180 (35⅞ × 70⅞). NGA/AC.

144 Jack Britten (Kija, b. c.1924). *Purnululu (Bull Creek country)*, 1988. Natural pigments on canvas 160 × 200 (63 × 78¾). NGA.

145 George Mung Mung (Kija, 1924–91). *Binoowoon country*, 1990. Natural pigments on canvas 80 × 160 (31½ × 63). NGA.

146 Detail of a rock wall, Emu Gallery, Laura, Queensland. Photo Percy Tresize. AIATSIS.

147 Unknown artist. Cardwell River, Queensland. Shield, collected 1897. Natural pigments on softwood h. 91 (35⅞). AM. Photo Carl Bento.

148 Unknown artist. Cardwell River, Queensland. Basket, 19th century. Natural pigments on lawyer cane h. 81.5 (32). MOV.

149 Arthur Koo'ekka Pambegan senior (1895–1972) and Arthur Koo'ekka Pambegan junior (b. 1936) (Wik-Mungkan). *Flying foxes*, 1962. Natural pigments on wood, fibre h. 129 (50¾). NMA.

150 Angus Namponan (Wik-Ngatharr, b. 1930) with Nelson Wolmby (Wik-Ngathan, b. 1951) and Peter Peemuggina (Wik-Ngathan, b. 1942). *Two Young Women of Cape Keerweer*, 1987. Wood, bark, natural pigments, nails, h. 70 (27⅝) and 73 (28¾). SAM.

151 Thancoupie (Thanaquith, b. 1937). *Garth Eran and Evarth Eran*. 1988. Stoneware h. 30.4 (12). NGA/AC.

152 Goobalathaldin (Dick Roughsey), (Lardil, 1924–85). *Rainbow Serpent, Thwiathu dance, Mornington Island*, 1972. Synthetic po-

lymer on board 31 × 41 (12¼ × 16⅛). NGA.

153 Kirk A. Watt (Lardil, b. c.1960). *Two stories*, 1991. Natural pigments on bark 67 × 37.5 (26⅜ × 14¾). Private Collection. Photo John Freund.

154 Unknown artist. East Torres Strait. *Krar (mask)*, 19th century. Turtleshell, hair, goa nuts, cassowary feathers, resin, fibres, ochres h. 47 (18½). AM. Photo John Fields.

155 Ken Thaiday (b. 1950). *Beizam (shark) dance mask*, 1991. Enamel on plastic and plywood, steel wire, dyed feathers, cockatoo feathers h. 70 (27⅝). NGA.

156 Jenuarrie (b. 1944). *Our time has begun*, 1986. Batik on cotton 217 × 197 (85⅜ × 77⅝). NGA.

157 William Barak (Woiwurrung, c.1824–1903). *Corroboree*, c.1885. Natural pigments and pencil on paperboard 56 × 75 (22 × 29½). NGA/AC.

158 Tommy McRae (Kwat Kwat?, 1836–1901). *A page from a sketchbook*, c.1890. Pen and ink on paper 20.2 × 16.2 (8 × 6⅜). NGA.

159 Alice Hinton-Bateup (b. 1950). *Dispossessed*, 1986. Poster: colour screenprint on paper 49.6 × 74.7 (19½ × 29⅜). NGA. Gift of Roger Butler 1985.

160 Kevin Gilbert (Wiradjuri, b. 1933). *My father's studio*, 1965, reprinted 1990. Linocut on paper 28.5 × 35.5 (11¼ × 14). NGA. Gordon Darling Fund 1990.

161 Avril Quaill (Nunukul, b. 1958). *Trespassers keep out*, 1982. Poster: colour screenprint on paper 48.7 × 72.1 (19⅛ × 28⅜). NGA.

162 James Simon (b. 1959). *Reflected images of heaven and earth*, 1991. Synthetic polymer on canvas 143 × 78 (56¼ × 30¾). The artist.

163 Trevor Nickolls (b. 1949). *Waterhole and trees*, 1986. Synthetic polymer on canvas 110.8 × 167.6 (43⅝ × 66). NGA. Philip Morris Arts Grant 1988.

164 Jeffrey Samuels (b. 1956). *This changing continent of Australia*, 1984. Oil on composition board 187 × 124 (73⅝ × 48⅞). AGNSW.

165 Michael Riley (b. 1960). *Christina*, 1986. Gelatin silver photograph 50 × 60 (19⅝ × 23⅝). The artist.

166 Brenda Croft (Kurindji, b. 1964). *Michael Watson in Redfern on the Long March of Freedom, Justice and Hope, Invasion Day, 26 January 1988, Sydney, NSW*, 1988. Gelatin silver photograph 50.5 × 40.5 (19⅞ × 16). NGA. KODAK (Australasia) PTY LTD Fund 1988.

167 Fiona Foley (Badtjala, b. 1964). *Annihilation of the blacks*, 1986. Wood, synthetic polymer, feathers, hair, rope h. 210 (82⅝). NMA.

168 Lin Onus (Wiradjuri, b. 1948). *Dingoes; dingo proof fence*, 1989 (detail from the series *Dingoes*). Synthetic polymer on fibreglass, wire, metal h. 95.5 (37½). NGA.

169 Euphemia Bostock (Bunjulung, b. 1936). *Possum skin print*, 1990. Screenprint on cotton 329.4 × 102.4 (129⅞ × 40⅜). NGA.

170 Bluey Roberts (b. 1937). *River spirit*,

1992. Carved emu egg h. 13 (5⅛). NGA.

171 Sally Morgan (b.1951). *Moon and stars*, 1987. Colour screenprint on paper 43 × 87.8 (16⅞ × 34⅝). The artist.

172 Bronwyn Bancroft (Bunjulung, b. 1958). *Cycle of life cape*, 1987. Hand-painted cotton h. 140 (55⅛). AM. Photo Carl Bento.

173 Arone Raymond Meeks (b. 1957). *Healing place*, 1988. Lithograph on paper 76 × 56.5 (29⅞ × 22⅛). The artist.

174 Byron Pickett (b. 1955). *Fellow Australian*, 1985. Colour screenprint on paper 55 × 51.2 (21⅝ × 20⅛). NGA.

175 Detail of 187 below.

176 Robert Campbell junior (Ngaku, b. 1944). *Aboriginal embassy*, 1986. Synthetic polymer on canvas 88 × 107.3 (34⅜ × 42¼). NGA.

177 Gordon Bennett (b. 1955). *Outsider*, 1988. Oil and synthetic polymer on canvas 290 × 180 (114⅛ × 70⅞). University of Queensland Museum of Modern Art, Brisbane.

178 Karen Casey (b. 1956). *Got the bastard*, 1991. Oil and mixed media on canvas 210 × 150 (82⅝ × 59). The artist.

179 Judy Watson (b. 1959). *Heartland*, 1991. Powder pigment, pastel on canvas 176 × 173.5 (69¼ × 68¼). NGA.

180 Ian W. Abdulla (Ngarrindjeri, b. 1947). *Sowing seeds at nite*, 1990. Synthetic polymer on canvas 100 × 100 (39⅜ × 39⅜). NGA. Moët et Chandon Fund.

181 Pooaraar (Bevan Hayward) (b. 1939). *Spirits of the Australian bushlands*, 1988. Linocut on paper 56 × 30 (22 × 11⅞). NGA/AC.

182 Treahna Hamm (Cummeragunja, b. 1965). *Rebirth II*, 1991. Etching on paper 74.8 × 34.2 (29½ × 13½). The artist.

183 Ricky Maynard (b. 1953). *Jason Thomas, Terry Maynard and David Maluga*, 1985. Gelatin silver photographs, each image 30 × 19.2 (11¾ × 7½). NGA.

184 Rick Roser (Jinibara, b. 1955). *Jundal gianga (woman powerful)*, 1990. Natural pigments and synthetic polymer on driftwood, string, feathers h. 155 (61). NGA.

185 Yvonne Koolmatrie (Ngarrindjeri, b. 1945). *Eel trap*, 1990. Sedge grass length 275 (108⅛). Tandanya Aboriginal Cultural Institute, Adelaide.

186 Richard Bell (Kamilaroi, b. 1953). *Crisis: what to do about this half-caste thing*, 1991. Synthetic polymer and collage on canvas 180 × 250 (70⅞ × 98⅜). NGA.

187 Paddy Dhatangu (Liyagalawumirri, b. 1915), David Malangi (Manharrngu, b. 1927), George Milpurrurru (Ganalbingu b. 1934), Jimmy Wululu (Daygurrgurr/Gupapuyngu, b. 1936) and other Ramingining artists. *The Aboriginal Memorial*, 1988 (an installation of 200 painted hollow-log coffins). Natural pigments on wood, from h. 40 (15¾) to 327 (128¾). NGA. Purchased with the assistance of funds from Gallery admission charges and commissioned in 1987.

213

Glossary

Main text references follow definitions. Numbers in *italic* refer to illustrations.

Awelye Women's designs and ceremonies (in the Anmatyerre language, spoken in the desert), 139, 142

Bradshaw figures Small, monochrome naturalistic human figures painted on rock walls in the Kimberley. Named after the explorer Captain Joseph Bradshaw, the first European to record such paintings in 1892, 157; *8*

Coolamon Wooden carrying dishes used in the desert, 97, 103, 114, 122, 129, 143; *104*

Dhulang Painted patterns or designs in North East Arnhem Land, 26, 59, 60, 65, 74

Dhuwa Name for one of the two complementary social and religious categories (moieties) in central and eastern Arnhem Land (see also Yirritja), 25, 42, 47–8, 51–2, 54, 56, 60, 65

Digging stick Long wooden stick used by women to gather roots and root vegetables, 32, 38, 45, 60, 99, 103, 143

Dilly bag Small bag, woven from natural fibre string, used in northern Australia for carrying food and personal possessions, and used in ceremonies, 14, 32, 38, 43–5, 54, 60, 74, 103; *29*

Dirmu Vibrant patterns found in nature and made in painting (in the Murrinh-Patha language, spoken in the Wadeye region), 94

Dreaming Term commonly used in Aboriginal Australia to refer to Aboriginal cosmology, encompassing the creator and ancestral beings, the laws of religious and social behaviour, the land, the spiritual forces which sustain life and the narratives which concern these (also called the Dreamtime), 10, 11, 15–16, 22, 47, 85, 93–4, 97, 99, 100, 107, 109

Dupun A Yolngu term for the hollow-log coffin (see below).

Hollow-log coffin Coffin made from a prepared and painted hollow log used in reburial ceremonies in Arnhem Land (the coffins are often called *lorrkon* in western

Arnhem Land), 59, 70, 74, 206; *175, 187*

Jukurrpa Dreaming (in Warlpiri, one of the languages spoken in the desert), 97

Kirda Among the Warlpiri and related desert groups, those with primary, usually patrilineally inherited rights in ceremonies, Dreamings, designs and so on (see also *kurdungurlu*), 100, 127, 130

Koori Generic term for the Aboriginal people of the south-eastern part of Australia (see also Murri, Nunga, Nyoongah), 179, 185–7

Kurdungurlu Among the Warlpiri and related desert groups, those with secondary, usually matrilineally inherited rights in ceremonies, Dreamings, graphic designs and so on (see also *kirda*), 100, 127, 130

Kuruwarri Men's designs and ceremonies (in the Warlpiri language), 99, 103

Macassans Fishermen and traders from Sulawesi in Indonesia, who visited the northern shores of the continent until the early twentieth century, 21, 23, 70, 72, 78, 81; *64*

Mimi Spirit figures that appear depicted on the rock walls of West Arnhem Land and Kakadu. Also refers to a style of painting which incorporates images of these spirits, 21–3, 27–8, 38, 47, 157; *12, 20*

Miny'tji Painted clan patterns or designs in central and north-eastern Arnhem Land, 25

Moiety One of a pair of complementary social and religious categories (see also Dhuwa and Yirritja), 15, 25, 42, 47, 54, 56–7, 66, 70, 100

Murri Generic term for the Aboriginal people of Queensland and northern parts of New South Wales, 179

Nunga Generic term for the Aboriginal people of the southern part of South Australia, 179

Nyoongah Generic term for the Aboriginal people of south-western Australia, 179, 195

Outstations Camps or settlements established by Aboriginal people on their traditional lands. Also known as homeland stations, 22, 66, 98, 139, 143

Palga Narrative dance cycle in the eastern Kimberley, in which performers carry painted boards or threaded-string constructions, 164–5

Pukumani State of mourning imposed upon the kin of a deceased person, and the name of the funeral ceremony among the Tiwi of Bathurst and Melville Islands, 85–9, 91; *69, 70–1*

Rainbow Serpent The name common in much of Aboriginal Australia for several supernatural beings in their manifestations as snakes (Wititj the Great Python etc.), 10, 22, 30–2, 34, 41, 47–50, 81, 84, 95, 120, 150, 161–4, 195; *16, 19, 21, 26, 80, 81, 103, 152, 171*

Rarrk Cross-hatched clan patterns in western Arnhem Land (see also *dhulang, dirmu,* and *miny'tji*), 25, 27, 30, 32, 34, 38, 41–3, 45, 172

Tingari Commonly described as a group of ancestral beings, with one or more dominant men or women, who brought law and culture to the peoples of the western desert region, 10, 112, 114, 147–8, 153–5

Wandjina Generic term for a group of ancestral beings in the Kimberley, who control the elements and maintain fertility in humans and other natural species, 10, 153, 157–61, 163–4, 168; *135, 136, 137*

Yawulyu Women's designs and ceremonies (in the Warlpiri language), 99, 103, 106, 130, 139

Yirritja Name for one of the two complementary social and religious categories (moieties) in central and eastern Arnhem Land (see also Dhuwa), 25, 42, 52, 56–7, 66, 70

Yolngu Generic term for the Aboriginal people of central and eastern Arnhem Land, 26, 47, 56–7, 59, 77, 82

Index